KATHY'S
GOOD NEWS

KATHY'S
GOOD NEWS

— WILSON AWASU

Outskirts Press, Inc.
Denver, Colorado

Outskirts Press, Inc.
http://www.outskirtspress.com

PB ISBN: 978-1-4327-6934-5
HB ISBN: 978-1-4327-6935-2

Outskirts Press and the "OP" logo are trademarks belonging to Outskirts Press, Inc.

PRINTED IN THE UNITED STATES OF AMERICA

"Promise you'll not laugh when I tell you what I want to say," Kathy said, looking worried. We sat facing each other in front of the pastor's desk.

I thought. *What does this twelve-year-old have to say? I've just finished a weeklong seminar on Life, Freedom and Power in her church. Women and men, and college and high school students said they've been spiritually renewed. Might it be that what I taught went over the heads of younger people? Would I know if I promise?*

"Kathy, I promise," I said.

"Thanks. Now, listen," she said. "I like what you said. But I'm glad you didn't ask people to come forward to receive Jesus."

"Why?"

"You still promise?"

"Yes."

"Okay. I would come forward, but I hate coming."

"Why?"

"That would be the tenth time," Kathy said and looked away, wiping tears from her cheeks.

When she turned round to look at me, I asked. "Why is that?"

"Don't you know? You're supposed to." She pulled forward to the edge of her seat, searching my eyes. She looked convinced that I knew what she was talking about.

Unfortunately, I had no clue. Should I take a guess?

"No, Kathy, I don't know what you're talking about."

"Okay, I'll tell you," she said, and sat back in her seat. "I don't think I understand the good news. If I did, I wouldn't go forward every time I hear it. Don't you think?"

I began to get it, but not quite. Who exactly is this twelve-year-old? How could I, a guest speaker, help her at the end of my series of talks?

"Tell me, Kathy. How can I help you?"

She stared at me for the longest moment and said, "Tell me the good news so that I get it. Isn't that what Jesus wants? Then I, too, can tell others, right?"

"Right."

Just then, Kathy's mom came in, saying it was time to go.

Kathy tore off the name and address page from her Bible and gave it to me. "Here," she said. "Write me." Her last look burned the saddest face of a twelve-year-old on my mind.

"I promise," I said.

All night long, and on my return flight to Minneapolis, Minnesota the next day, I saw that face captioned: "Tell me the good news so that I get it."

Kathy's e-mail reached my office before I did.

Date: 3/5/07
Subject: Kathy's good news
From: Kathy
To: Doctor Wilson

Dear Doctor,
I think Mom was rude to you when she called me away last night. Please forgive her. They looked for me everywhere. Mom was going to work at 11 p.m. That's why.
Well, don't forget my request. I call it Kathy's good news, if that's okay. Let me hear from you soon. Thanks.
Your friend,
Kathy.

Subject: Kathy's good news
Date: 3/6/07
From: Doctor Wilson
To: Kathy

Dear Kathy,

I have nothing to forgive your mom. I hope she got to work on time Sunday night.

Sure, Kathy. I think "Kathy's good news" is a good title for our discussion. But before we start, tell me more about how you feel about yourself, family, church, and school. Okay?

Your friend,
Doctor Wilson.

Date: 3/7/07
Subject: Kathy's good news
From: Kathy
To: Doctor Wilson

Dear Doctor,

I don't see how my feelings about myself and family and church and the school I go to relate to Kathy's good news. But you know what you're doing. So I'll tell you.

Me: I think I'm not a Christian yet. I have gone forward nine times to receive Christ. And as I told you if you had invited people forward at the end of your talks, I would have come. Why that many times? I read my Bible. I pray. I go to church.

I try to obey Daddy and Mom. I also try to be good to my brother and sister. But it's hard to forgive them when they're mean to me. Both of them are leaders in the youth group at church. They're supposed to know better. But they don't.

If I were a Christian I should forgive them, right? But how about them, they're Christian. Why doesn't it bother them when they mistreat their younger sister? I feel bad about bad things I do. Why don't they?

Oops, I began to talk about how I feel about my family without telling you I've started. Anyway, I am the youngest of three children. I thought parents and brothers and sisters spoil youngest kids. How come I'm not? Daddy doesn't allow me to spend a night out with friends. He only allows me to invite Pat over once a while. She's my best friend.

We live in a 6-bedroom house with five bathrooms. Daddy

and Mom should hire a housekeeper, but no. We all clean house, even me. I wonder what Daddy and Mom do with all the money they make. Daddy is President of a computer company. Mom is an ICU Nurse at Huntington Memorial Hospital. Where does the money go? I wish I knew.

Oh, I know. Daddy gives a lot of it to the church. That brings me to how I feel about church. Daddy and Mom are church elders. Are church elders supposed to give lots of money? Well, our church has 2,000 members, so I'm told. I don't know how many elders we have. But I know we have six pastors.

Mom says I embarrass the family when I keep going forward to receive Christ. But I can't help it when I haven't received him yet. And that's why I sometimes don't like going to church.

Preachers often talk about being born again, accept Christ, receive Jesus, repent, and stuff like that. I want to do it and get it done. But then I feel sad for embarrassing the family. So I have a secret wish when I'm going to church. I pray the preacher wouldn't use those words or invite people forward. It's bad to pray like that, isn't it?

School: I feel better at school. Though it's the church school, the born again stuff doesn't come up that much. My most favorite teacher is Mrs. Foster. She's pretty. And she's a good teacher. She says religion is a matter of the heart, as it should be.

Doc, I wonder. Is this an essay or what? Anyway, I've told you a lot of things. But please don't let this stuff get in the way of telling me the good news so I get it. That's the important thing.

Love,

Kathy.

Subject: Kathy's good news
Date: 3/8/07
From: Doctor Wilson
To: Kathy

Hello Kathy,

Superb! You've given me a clearer picture of you and your situation. Below is my summary of what you said.

You belong to an upper middle-class family, a Christian home, and a large suburban church. And you go to a Christian school. But you desire a personal relationship with God beyond

- the comfort of a well to do family, and
- the upbringing of a Christian home.

I'm proud of you for not hiding that desire. I'm also proud of you, Kathy, for showing me that you feel lost at church. So I'm thinking

- you want clear understanding to remove the confusion that your church experience has given you
- you want a heart experience of God beyond the head knowledge you now have about God
- you want to have a personal relationship

with God and be sure about it instead of being unsure about it.

Tell me, Kathy, if that's it, thanks.
Love,
Doctor Wilson.

Date: 3/8/07
Subject: Kathy's good news
From: Kathy
To: Doctor Wilson

Dear Doctor,
Wow. That's exactly what I want. I'm excited. Can we start talking about Kathy's good news now?
Your friend,
Kathy.

Subject: Kathy's good news
Date: 3/9/07
From: Doctor Wilson
To: Kathy

Dear Kathy,
Yes, yes, we'll start talking about Kathy's good news in a moment. But before then, you and I need to

take a good look at feeling lost at church in terms of

- people-lostness
- origin of lostness, and
- Jesus and lostness.

A thorough understanding of those issues is foundational to Kathy's good news.

Give me ten days and I'll get back to you.

Your friend,

Doctor Wilson.

Subject: Kathy's good news
Date: 3/23/07
From: Doctor Wilson
To: Kathy

Hey Kathy,

Thanks for your patience. It's taken me two weeks to get back to you. But during that time, I went back to study Jesus' teaching on people-lostness in Luke 15:1-24 (see the attached file on people-lostness). The teaching says it doesn't matter whether the lost

- are unconscious that they're lost
- are conscious and care about it or don't care they're lost, or

- brought it on themselves, that is, they chose to be lost.

Lost is lost, because being lost is disconnection from God. Most lost people are content to live free, independent of God.

Find more about this in the attached, thanks.

Love,

Doctor Wilson.

Attachment file to 3/23/07 e-mail

People Lostness

In Luke 15:1-24, see passage below, Jesus used imageries of the lost sheep, the lost coin, and the lost son, to teach about people lostness.

1 Now the tax collectors and sinners were all drawing near to hear him. 2 And the Pharisees and the scribes murmured, saying, "This man receives sinners and eats with them."

3 So he told them this parable: 4 "What man of you, having a hundred sheep, does not leave the ninety-nine in the wilderness, and go after the one which is lost, until he finds it? 5 And when he has found it, he lays it on his shoulders,

rejoicing. 6 And when he comes home, he calls together his friends and his neighbors, saying to them, 'Rejoice with me, for I have found my sheep which was lost.' 7 Just so, I tell you, there will be more joy in heaven over one sinner who repents than over ninety-nine righteous persons who need no repentance.

8 "Or what woman, having ten coins, if she loses one coin, does not light a lamp and sweep the house and seek diligently until she finds it? 9 And when she has found it, she calls together her friends and neighbors, saying, 'Rejoice with me, for I have found the coin which I had lost.' 10 Just so, I tell you, there is joy before the angels of God over one sinner who repents."

11 And he said, "There was a man who had two sons; and the younger one of them said to his father, 'Father, give me the share of property that falls to me.' And he divided his living between them. 13 Not many days later, the younger son gathered all he had and took his journey into a far country, and there he squandered his property in loose living. 14 And when he had spent everything, a great famine arose in that country, and he began to be in want. 15 So he went and joined himself to one of the citizens of that country, who sent him into his fields to feed swine. 16 And he would gladly have fed on the pods that the swine ate; and no one gave him anything.

17 "But when he came to himself he said, 'How many of my father's hired servants have bread enough and to spare, but I perish here with hunger! 18 I will arise and go to my father, and I will say to him, "Father, I have sinned against heaven and before you; 19 I am no longer worthy to be called your son; treat me as one of your hired servants."'"

20 "And he rose and came to his father. But while he was yet at a distance, his father saw him and had compassion, and ran and embraced him and kissed him. 21 And the son said to him, 'Father, I have sinned against heaven and before you; I am no longer worthy to be called your son.' 22 But the father said to his servants, 'Bring quickly the best robe, and put it on him; and put a ring on his hand, and shoes on his feet; 23 and bring the fatted calf and kill it, and let us eat and make merry; 24 for this my son was dead and is alive again; he was lost, and is found.' And they began to make merry."

The lost sheep (verses 1-7)

The lost sheep strayed from the flock and shepherd. It was lost and it knew it. It might bleat for attention. So the lost sheep represents "conscious lostness."

The lost coin (verses 8-10)

The lost coin on the other hand dropped from the owner's hand. And it rolled away, buried under furniture or clutter in a room. It was also lost. But because it was metal, a non-living thing, it didn't know it was lost. Therefore the lost coin represents "unconscious lostness."

The lost son (verses 11-24)

Unlike the lost sheep and the lost coin, the lost son was a person. He chose to leave home and be gone from home, free to live as he pleased, unbothered by his mom or dad. He chose to be lost. The lost son, then, represents "willful lostness."

Date: 3/23/07
Subject: Kathy's good news
From: Kathy
To: Doctor Wilson

Hi Doc,

I was getting anxious when your deadline passed and I didn't hear from you. But I said I'd wait. I'm glad I did.

I've heard many sermons on the lost. But I've never seen lostness as disconnection from God. And the disconnected, the lost, are content to live independent of God? That's scary. I think

I get it but I don't. Please, tell me more about "lostness" and "disconnection from God."

Hey, Doc, I told my best friend, Pat, about you. Can I share your e-mails with her?

Take care,

Kathy.

Subject: Kathy's good news

Date: 4/6/07

From: Doctor Wilson

To: Kathy

Sure, Kathy, share my e-mails with Pat. And tell her I say Hi.

Find attached a document titled "Unconscious and conscious lostness." You'll see that I've broadly divided the lost into two groups, one, unconscious lostness, and two, conscious lostness. Each group sub-divides into three.

The groups and sub-groups are examples of lost people. But I hope they give you a good picture of people-lostness, or disconnectedness from God. Tell me what you think after you've gone through the document. Thanks.

Your friend,

Doctor Wilson.

Attachment file to 4/6/07 e-mail

Unconscious and Conscious Lostness

Lostness is disconnection from God. The disconnected or lost live independently of God. That is living without conscious awareness of God. The attitude is, "Leave me alone to do as I please." Broadly speaking, lostness or disconnection divides into

- being unconsciously lost or disconnected from God, and
- being consciously lost or disconnected from God

The unconsciously lost split into

- occult-controlled victims
- religion-controlled victims
- mind-controlled victims, etc.

a. Occult-controlled victims

Occult-controlled victims grow up in occult homes and read occult books from childhood. They also watch occult related videos and play computerized occult games. And maybe they dabble with tarot cards and ouija-boards. They consult palm-readers, psychic counselors, channelers, TM, etc.

b. Religion-controlled victims

Religion-controlled victims are raised on religious views that say gods live out there. Seek them and worship them. Worshiping them draws them closer so they can offer answers on some of life's tough questions. Another view says that there's god in everyone. Get to know the god within, and you have no need for a god out there.

c. Mind-controlled victims

Mind-control victims grow up breathing and drinking insistence on running everything through the grid of "What makes sense." What makes sense is real and important. What doesn't make sense isn't real. Therefore it's not important.

All these are lost. They live independent of God but don't know it. Or they do but they don't care about it.

The consciously lost divide into

- unsaved worshippers of God
- false starts, and
- willful haters of God, etc.

a. Unsaved worshipers of God

Unsaved worshipers of God know about God. They consciously worship him. They're moralists, do-gooders. But they remain unsaved because their knowledge about God and worship of God lack a knowledge of Jesus.

b. False starts

False starts know about God (and sometimes about Jesus). They might grow up in Christian homes. Therefore they read the Bible and pray. But they, too, are unsaved. Here's their biggest problem. They lack experience of the things they believe and are trying hard to do. There's a big gap between their head and heart, knowledge and experience.

c. Willful haters of God

Unlike the false starts and unsaved worshipers of God, willful haters of God choose on purpose to go away from God and Jesus. Some of them might have served God as pastors or missionaries. But somewhere, somehow, they feel disappointed in God.

For example, God let 4-year-old Melissa die after they'd prayed and waited 15 years for her. Or they've served God faithfully, yet God let their dreams, plans and efforts for success and recognition blow up. They blame God for it all. He "let them down." So they desert him to pay him back for failing them.

Others are kids brought up as 'Christian.' They knew and did all the right things. But they didn't have a personal relationship with God while growing up. In adulthood their childhood worship of God makes no sense to them. So, they toss the faith of their parents and go looking for some religious experience that makes sense.

In spite of the differences, the consciously lost and the

unconsciously lost live disconnected from God. They all need reconnection to God.

Date: 4/6/07
Subject: Kathy's good news
From: Kathy
To: Doctor Wilson

Hi Doc,

Pat was here spending the night when I opened your e-mail. We read it together. I'm a false start. But know what, now I wonder why I read the Bible, and pray, and go to church, and try so hard to be good?

I know Daddy is a no-nonsense man. Mom is too, but in her own way, if you see what I mean.

I wonder. Do I do it all to please them? Don't tell me. Let me think. I think that's it.

Pat isn't like me. She has a spirit guide, she told me. She said her parents practice the occult. She and her sister, five years older, wear a crystal around their neck. Pat doesn't remember when she started watching horror movies and playing occult related video games.

The kind of family you grow up in has a lot to do with it, like Pat and me, right? Okay, Doc, please tell me how I can experience what I know about God and Jesus.

Love,
Kathy.

Date: 4/7/07
Subject: Kathy's good news
From: Kathy
To: Doctor Wilson

Doc, it's me again. I can't stop reading your document on 'Unconscious and Conscious Lostness.' It's full of good stuff. The stuff about willful haters of God is getting me. I can see why someone can become like that. Who wants to go on worshiping God when worshiping God becomes meaningless?

I'm scared. I may become like that. I don't want to. What do you think?

Okay Doc, bye,
Kathy.

Date: 4/8/07
Subject: Kathy's good news
From: Kathy
To: Doctor Wilson

Hi Doctor,

I hope you don't mind three e-mails, one after the other? I just have to tell you. You've got me thinking. Can you please add this to what you'll be telling me? How did lostness come to be a problem for everyone? Thanks.

Your friend,
Kathy.

Subject: Kathy's good news
Date: 4/11/07
From: Doctor Wilson
To: Kathy

Hello Kathy,

No, I don't mind reading three e-mails from you all at once.

Good for you, Kathy. You see yourself as a false start. You do all your Christian duties to please your mom and dad. But I think going forward again and again to receive Jesus at church is more than that.

It seems to me, deep down, you desire to know God in a personal way. And because you haven't yet, you keep going forward looking for it. That desire shows an awareness of being disconnected from God. The need to get back to God began at the time people-lostness began. You'll see how it all fits together in the attached file titled "Origin of lostness."

I hope our discussions will help you to enter a personal relationship with God. Then you wouldn't become a willful hater of God later in life.

Okay, Kathy, hurry to the attached and see what it says.

Your friend,
Doctor Wilson.

Attachment file to 4/11/07 e-mail

Origin of Lostness

Being lost began with Eve and Adam's rebellion against God (Genesis 3). That rebellion is also called sin. When Eve and Adam sinned against God, they lost their God-given ability to think godly thoughts, for example, holy, righteous, clean, pure, selfless thoughts. Inability to think in a godly way prevented them from acting godly, e.g., to love, to be kind, to forgive, to trust God, or to be humble.

But Eve and Adam's loss of God-given ability to think godly and act godly also resulted in an inability to resist or say no to ungodly thinking and ungodly acts. That's bondage.

In a moment of rebellion, sin, Eve and Adam went

- from being God-like to being unlike God
- from obedience and friendship with God to disobedience and enmity with God
- from living dependent on God to living independent of God, and
- from life to death.

Death is separation or disconnection from God.

There are three types of death. The first is living physically but living dead or insensitively to God. It's living independently of God, bothered or unbothered about it. The second is dying physically. That's when the human spirit leaves the body.

The third death separates the dead, body and spirit, from God forever. Living independently of God earns the state of spiritual death: living forever separated from God.

Eve and Adam passed all that on to their descendants. From that time on, all human beings are born dead. And born dead, it's natural for all human beings to desire and insist to be let alone to do as they please.

Tragically, that desire comes naturally to people. But its implications and outcomes remain hidden to them. For example, people don't know that they're enslaved to the desire and insistence to be let alone to live as they please. The enslavement makes them enemies of God.

Therefore they deserve God's punishment for living independently of God. They, in fact, earn God's punishment to be forever separated, body and spirit, from him when they physically die.

Since all human beings descend from Eve and Adam, they take on the likeness of Eve and Adam. They're all unlike God. They're lost. No human being, Noah, Abraham, Moses, Peter, Paul, or Mother Teresa, is good enough to do anything to reverse their doom. Only God could act to change the situation. Did he? What did he do? And how did he do it?

Date: 4/13/07
Subject: Kathy's good news
From: Kathy
To: Doctor Wilson

Dear Doctor,

In the last minute Pat called to cancel coming to spend the night. I miss her. But I need time alone to take care of the headache your teaching on the "Origin of Lostness" gave me. Not that I don't like what you said. I do.

But it's full of serious stuff. For example, this is the first time I see that we're powerless against the desire to be let alone to do as we please. All of us. Wow!

And all the bad things we do come from that desire. It's scary that we can neither avoid the results now nor in the future. Thanks for showing me all this. That's a lot to think about.

Now, Doc, please help me with this thought. I thought God is all-powerful. How come Satan has the power of death? Hebrews 2:14 says he does. God can't have it at the same time Satan has it, right?

Your friend,

Kathy.

Subject: Kathy's good news
Date: 4/14/07
From: Doctor Wilson
To: Kathy.

Dear Kathy,

It's always a joy to hear from you. I'm glad you find my teaching on the origin of lostness helpful. You asked a good question. How could God be all-powerful when Satan had the power of death? We could write a book on that. But I'll be brief.

[By the way, did you see that I changed the tense from "has" to "had"? Satan did have the power of death. He doesn't anymore.]

God was all-powerful even when Satan had the power of death. Satan (a fallen angel) like all fallen angels and loyal angels, plus people, animals, the sun, the moon, the stars, and all creation owe

- their lives (existence), and
- their power (force, strength)

to God. He's the Creator of all things (Genesis 1-2).

But God didn't have the power associated with death when Satan had it. This explains: Like Gabriel and Michael, Lucifer too was a loyal angel. He became Satan when he rebelled against God. That happened before the creation of Adam and Eve.

That was when Satan invented sin, disobedience, rebellion against God. Death, separation or disconnection from God, resulted from that sin. And since sin began with Satan, logically, the power connected with sin and death must belong to Satan.

But through his death and resurrection, Jesus defeated Satan and that power. He took the power of sin and death from Satan since that point.

"Don't be afraid," Jesus said to John in AD 95

when John was in exile to Patmos Island. "I am the First and the Last. I am the living one who died. Look, I am alive forever and ever! And I hold the keys [the power] of death and the grave" (Rev. 1:17-18, compare Isa. 14:12-21, Luke 22:69, Rom. 5:12, 6:23, Eph. 1:19-23).

If Satan had known that he'd lose the power of death to Jesus in Jesus' crucifixion, he wouldn't have allied with Judas, the Pharisees and Pilate to crucify Jesus (Luke 22:3-6). As it was, he didn't know. God hid it from him (1 Cor. 2:8; compare 1 John 3:8).

That's it for now, Kathy.

Your friend,

Doctor Wilson.

Date: 4/14/07

Subject: Kathy's good news

From: Kathy

To: Doctor Wilson

Hello Doctor,

Thanks a lot for your answer to my question. Now, please tell me more about how Jesus defeated Satan, sin and death. Thanks.

Your friend,

Kathy.

Subject: Kathy's good news
Date: 4/18/07
From: Doctor Wilson
To: Kathy

Dear Kathy,

I apologize if the attached document is too long. I also apologize if you have to look up some words in a dictionary. But, you know, I want to give you a sound biblical answer to your question, "How did Jesus defeat Satan, sin and death?"

Before reading the attached, read Isaiah 61:1-2 three times in your Bible. Then jump to Luke 4:1-30 and read it once. Return to verses 18-19 and read them two times. That's background reading for the attached.

Take your time to read the attached and tell me if the material answers your question.

Your friend,
Doctor Wilson.

Attachment document to 4/18/07 e-mail

Jesus and Lostness

Hebrews 2:14-18 says,

> Because God's children are human beings—made of flesh
> and blood—Jesus also became flesh and blood by being
> born in human form. For only as a human being could he
> die, and only by dying could he break the power of the
> Devil, who had the power of death. Only in this way could
> he deliver those who have lived all their lives as slaves of
> the fear of dying....

That says Jesus could only die in human form. And
only in dying to resurrect could he

- defeat Satan, sin and death, and their controlling
  power on people, and
- free people who repent and confess enslavement
  to the power of Satan, sin and death (Heb. 2:14-15
  compare 1 John 3:8).

In dying, Jesus absorbed death into himself and con-
verted it into life-giving power. As a direct result, his resurrection represents our re-creation.

Our re-creation gives us spiritual, mental, emotional,
and physical wholeness we never had. Therefore our re-
creation is freedom from

- enslavement to our rebellion against God and punishment for it, and
- enslavement to Satan and all evil forces and trends that exploit our enslavement to our rebellion against God.

Jesus put it like this. "No one can enter a strong man's house and plunder his goods, unless he first binds the strong man; then indeed he may plunder his house," (Mark 3:27). The "strong man" is Satan. And Jesus is the "stronger-man," who had indeed defeated Satan to free us from our lifelong bondage to the fear of dying.

That also makes Jesus our only freedom from

- the power of Satan, and
- the power of the fear of dying (Heb. 2:14-15 compare Rev. 12:11).

The result is that Jesus is

- the provider of re-connection to God, and
- the re-connection to God.

As reconnector to God, Jesus is,

- good news to the poor
- release for the captives
- sight for the blind, and

- freedom for the oppressed (Isa. 61:1-2 compare Luke 4:18-19).

Jesus as good news to the poor

The poor here describes us as we are when we live independently of God. Our poverty is our inability

- to think godly
- to act godly, and
- to say no to thinking ungodly and acting ungodly

plus

- our enslavement to the power of Satan, sin and death, and
- our being guilty before God because of our inability and enslavement.

Therefore, our poverty disconnects all of us from God. It makes us worthy of one thing, being forever separated from God. That is to live separated from God, body and spirit, forever and ever. Since our poverty affects all of us, none of us could do anything to change

- our loss of God-likeness
- our enslavement for losing our God-likeness, and
- our punishment for losing our God-likeness and

being enslaved to that loss.

That's bad news.

But there's good news. The good news is Jesus. Being God in human form, Jesus outmatched our poverty, our spiritual bankruptcy, with his richness. He lived a sinless life. He lived depending on God the Father, obeying him in everything and in every way (John 5:19, 30, 8:29).

Then he met and defeated Satan, sin and death through his death. His resurrection, ascension and enthronement are proof of that. And that makes Jesus good news to us, the spiritually bankrupt, as well as reconnection to God. But that's not all.

Jesus as release to the captives

People's inability to think and act godly enslaves them. This means that the desire to be let alone to live as one pleases is actually a trap, a form of imprisonment. Living imprisoned that way makes people think that they're in charge of their lives. They feel confident that they make their own decisions and choices to do or not do this or that.

Unfortunately, it's the enslavement to

- the power of sin
- the power of Satan, and
- the power of death

that's in charge.

They lose the power to say no to forces stronger than they are the moment they choose to be let alone to do as they please. Those forces control living independently of God. They come from satanic moral codes made up of

- defiance (rebellion)
- force (vigorous compelling or seductive compelling)
- greed (inability to know when enough is enough)
- selfishness (inflated concern for oneself and no concern for others), and
- evil ambition (desire to be #1 at all costs).

Eve and Adam accessed those moral codes when they listened to Satan and rebelled against God in the Garden of Eden (Gen. 3).

Being falsely confident that they are in charge when they are not makes individuals helpless and hopeless captives of those moral codes. The moral codes lure them to kill them and destroy them. That hardens them toward God. The hardness convinces them God is a killjoy. And it leads them to stay away from him. They sense the urging: "You can find joy and fulfillment on your own. Go for it."

But sadly, whatever joy people find away from God, entangles them. It exploits them, leaving them dissatisfied like the prodigal son (Luke 15:11-20). That's captivity from which only Jesus is the release. His death, resurrection, ascension and enthronement defeated the captivity, and took power over it. That makes Jesus the release for captives as well as sight for the blind.

Jesus as sight to the blind

Being spiritually blind, unable to understand spiritual views of things, is a direct result of our spiritual poverty, bankruptcy and captivity. Our poverty blinds us to the moral codes that control living independently of God.

And our blindness builds cataracts. The cataracts reverse our view of morality. They screw us up. So we see

- the good as bad, the bad as good
- the right as wrong, the wrong as right
- the true as untrue, and the untrue as true.

For example, when our reasoning is screwed up, it makes perfect sense to us that God is a killjoy. He doesn't love us. He can't love us or care for us. Maybe he doesn't even exist. We can take care of ourselves. Just as we know what clothes to buy and we buy them, we also can plan our lives ten, twenty years ahead, and work our way forward accordingly without any thought of God.

Should disaster strike, we explain it away, taking disaster as a normal part of life. That's the way it's supposed to be. But just as we're helpless against the unexpected and unpredictable, we're also helpless against distorted views of God and others and ourselves and our circumstances. We live in suspicion of God and people.

In that helplessness and hopelessness Jesus comes as hope and help and peace. He comes as sight for the blind. Why? He not only defeated the moral codes that run affairs in living independent of God. He gives release, sight, and freedom to victims who repent.

Jesus as freedom for the oppressed

People who live without God earn a life forever separated, body and spirit, from God. They often avoid talking about that reality while alive. Unfortunately, at death, they have to face the reality and live with it forever.

But that reality doesn't wait until death to oppress people. All through life it pokes victims in the form of inexplicable dissatisfaction and restlessness, fear and uncertainty, distrust and anxiety that even the wealthy and healthy, the famous and powerful, feel from time to time. Nothing can be more oppressive than that!

The goodness of the good news is this. The Jesus, who is tomorrow's judge is today's freedom. He said, "If the Son shall set you free, you shall be free indeed," (John 8:36). Seven hundred years before Jesus, Isaiah also said that about Jesus (Isaiah 61:1-2). Jesus quoted Isaiah to confirm the fact in a Synagogue at Nazareth (Luke 4:18-19).

Jesus is indeed our freedom, sight, release, and good news. Why? Jesus, the sinless one, made himself sin in his crucifixion, and God the Father punished him as sin deserves.

Date: 4/18/07
Subject: Kathy's good news
From: Kathy
To: Doctor Wilson.

Dear Doctor,

Thank you; thank you, for expanding my understanding of how Jesus defeated Satan. I'm going to read and read and read and keep reading your teaching. There's a lot to learn from it. For now, I can tell you this. My heart bubbles with love for Jesus.

I don't know exactly why. Is it because I now see Jesus as the giver of good news, and as the good news itself? And he is our freedom too. Can you help me to understand what's happening to me? I'm about to explode with joy. Thanks

Your friend,
Kathy.

Subject: Kathy's good news
Date: 4/20/07
From: Doctor Wilson

To: Kathy.

Dear Kathy,

Falling in love with Jesus is the best thing that can happen to anyone. I'm glad your heart is bubbling with love for Jesus. Hang loose and let it explode. And keep basking in the explosion. You'll find in the attached file some biblical examples of people who responded to Jesus' love for them exactly like that. I think you'll find them inspiring.

Okay, Kathy, bye for now,
Doctor Wilson.

Attachment file to 4/20/07 e-mail

Biblical Examples of Reconnection to God

The legion demoniac

In Gadarenes, Jesus met an unusual man. This man wore no clothes, and lived in cemeteries. He often cried while cutting himself with sharp stones. To protect him from himself, jailers often chained him and put fetters on him. But he was so strong; he broke the chains and disconnected the fetters. He escaped from jail, and left town to hang out in nearby cemeteries.

One day he met Jesus on a trail. He ran and fell at his feet. Jesus ejected demons from him and they filled 2,000 pigs grazing nearby. The pigs ran amok and drowned in a lake. The man returned to sanity at once. He wanted to follow Jesus when he left the area. But Jesus wouldn't let him.

Instead he told him, "Go home to your friends and tell them how much the Lord has done for you, and how he has had mercy on you" (Mark 5:19).

The exorcised man went to the Ten-Towns and told how much Jesus had done for him. The people recognized him as the former legion demoniac. And they marveled at how different he'd become, and at all the things he said about Jesus (Mark 5:1-20)

Zacchaeus the chief tax collector

Then there was Zacchaeus, the chief tax collector. Society disliked him and looked down on him as we do AIDS patients today. One day he heard Jesus coming up a street arched with trees. Because he was a short man, he climbed one of those trees to see Jesus unhindered by the crowd.

When Jesus reached there, he stood beneath the tree, looked up and said. "Zacchaeus, quick, quick, come down, for I must stay in your house today" (Luke 19:5). He climbed down and gave Jesus a dinner. Present with them were Jesus' disciples and many tax collectors Zacchaeus had invited to meet Jesus.

In the course of dinner, Zacchaeus got up and said, "Master, I'll give half my income to the poor. And I'll pay back four times people I've cheated through inflated taxation," (Luke 19:8)

"Today," Jesus said, "salvation has come to this home." (Luke 19:9, compare verses 1-10).

Mary Magdalene

Then we're told that Jesus exorcised Mary Magdalene of seven demons. Later we hear that she and Joanna, the wife of Chuza, Herod's steward, and Susanna, and many other women financially supported Jesus. And Mary Magdalene was the first person to see Jesus on the resurrection morning (Luke 8:1-3 compare Mark 16:1-11 and John 20:1-18).

The Samaritan woman

John talks about a Samaritan woman Jesus met at Jacob's well in Sychar.

"Give me a drink of water," Jesus said to her (John 4:7).

"How can you, a Jew, ask me for a drink of water?" The woman protested because a Jew wouldn't drink from a cup a Samaritan had drunk from (John 4:9).

In spite of that, Jesus chatted with her about issues from Samaritan culture and Jewish culture, Jewish worship of God in the temple and Samaritan worship of God on Mount Sinai, and personal lifestyle issues. The woman raised the issues. Jesus answered in order to tell her about reconnection to God.

The Samaritan woman seemed impressed by this male Jew, who broke social taboos and chatted with her. But she didn't seem convinced by everything he said. So she said, "I know that Messiah is coming. When he comes he'll tell us who's right and who's wrong on the issues," (John 4:25).

"I who speak with you am he," Jesus said, staring at her (John 4:26).

The woman's lower jaw nearly hit the ground. She left her water jar at the well, and ran to invite her townspeople to Jesus. After listening to Jesus, they said to her, "At first we believed because of your testimony. But after hearing Jesus ourselves, we know. He is indeed the Savior of the world," (John 4:42, compare verses 1-42).

Date: 4/20/07
Subject: Kathy's good news
From: Kathy
To Doctor Wilson

Dear Doctor,
I like those stories. Thanks. But I'm wondering, and forgive me, Doctor, if this is rude. Can you tell me your personal story?

Please, tell me how you personally experienced Jesus. Tell me everything, okay? I can't wait.
Your friend,
Kathy.

Subject: Kathy's good news
Date: 4/22/07
From: Doctor Wilson
To: Kathy

Okay, okay, Kathy, find attached my personal experience of Jesus. I hope you like it.
Your friend,
Doctor Wilson.

Attachment file to 4/22/07 e-mail

My Personal Experience of Reconnection to God

My own experience of reconnection to God happened late afternoon, on the second Thursday in March. Mom took me for a walk in a coconut grove at the east end of town in Ghana. I'd just turned ten. Mom stared at me as we walked along and said,

"Son, do you know God in a personal way?"

Anyone but Mom could ask me that question. Because Mom, more than anyone else, knew that Sunday was the high point in my childhood week. I was in church before the third and last church bell tolled at 9:30 a.m.. When it stopped, it said the pastor and choir were at the door to the sanctuary. The congregation stood to receive them.

The choir robed in black gowns, with white collars for ladies, and hip-length white surplices for men, entered the sanctuary. They walked down the center aisle in two lines, singing like angels: "Jesus shall reign wherever the sun..." The pastor followed three paces behind them, robed in clericals.

Five paces to the altar, one line turned left circling the altar clockwise. The other went right circling the altar counterclockwise. The lines merged into the first six pews in front to the right near the organ, standing.

The pastor stood in front of the altar facing the congregation. A hush settled. Then he trumpeted a Psalm. The choir replied with a doxology and sat down. The congregation followed. Usual church rituals took their rightful place and the choir and pastor recessed, singing like angels again. The worship service ended. I ached for next time.

Did Mom, in a keen mother-fashion, catch the ache and know what it meant in a religious son? Was that why she asked, "Do you know God in a personal way?"

She must have. Unsatisfied with my puzzled look, she went ahead and told me how, using Nicodemus as an example (John 3).

"Nicodemus was a ruler of the Jews, a teacher of God's word and a good man," Mom started. "But Jesus told him, 'You must be born spiritually to live spiritually.'"

I thought. That means, aside from my ten-year Christian upbringing I also need to be born spiritually to live spiritually.

"How?" I asked

"As human beings," Mom said. "We all like to be let alone to do as we please. That's what it means to be human. And that's what makes us all sinners, because all our acts of sin come from that desire. Do you understand?"

"Yes, no, um, no. Tell me, Mom."

"Wanting to be let alone to do as one pleases is rebellion against God, our Maker," Mom said. "It's telling God, we own our lives. We know what life is all about. We know better. We don't need God."

I thought. How can anyone not need God? What can we do right without him? We all need God, all the time.

"Mom," I said, "that's bad, very bad indeed. What can we do about that?"

"Repent for being like that," she said. "And believe that Jesus died so that you won't die, that is, live forever without God, for being a sinner."

"I do with all my heart," I said.

"Good. Now, ask God to forgive you and free you from the hold and dirt of sin."

I pictured the "hold" and "dirt" of sin as being trapped helpless and hopeless to do right. It was nice to know that

God wanted to do something about it. But I wasn't sure he would.

"Mom," I asked, "are you sure he will?"

"Certainly. God did not only promise he would. Right now, he's waiting to forgive you, free you, and enter your life. Accept his forgiveness, and welcome him into your life. Trust him. He means business. And he enters your life the moment you ask him."

Just like that, huh? There was no lightning or thunder when I did. But instantly I knew peace and freedom I'd never known. The next few days I devoured Mark, Luke, Matthew and John, with new meaning and delight. Seven months later I shared the experience with my Dad. He experienced God the way I did right then. Three days later he died.

Initially his sudden death shocked and saddened me, and maybe made me angry with God. But right then a passion to nudge church people (like Dad) to be sure they know God in a personal way seized me. I climbed trees and rooftops at dawn, sang and preached two-minute sermons.

Sometimes when I climbed down, I met people gathered to check out if I were an angel. Sharing the joy, peace, freedom and power found in a personal relationship with God became a lifestyle for me ever since.

Date: 4/22/07
Subject: Kathy's good news
From: Kathy
To: Doctor Wilson

Dear Doctor,

I like your mom. I want her for a pen-pal, please. And know what, Doc? I'll like to be like her when I grow up. Then I'll have a son like you.

I liked the conversion stories of the Samaritan woman, Mary Magdalene, Zacchaeus and the legion demoniac a lot. But yours tops them all. You know why? You and I are kindred spirits. Like me, you too were a false start. But God changed you when you experienced him in a personal way. I want to experience God the way you did. Please tell me how.

And, hey Doc, don't forget to give me your mom's contact links.

Love,
Kathy.

Subject: Kathy's good news
Date: 4/26/07
From: Doctor Wilson
To: Kathy

Dear Kathy,

I wish my Mom could hear your compliments of

her. But maybe she can't from where she is. She died when I was in grad school in Pasadena, California. So I accept your compliments on her behalf. I'm flattered that you see her as a role model. Thanks.

But know what? You're already behaving like her. You're doing for yourself what she did for me. She refused to take it that my Christian upbringing made me a child of God. She took steps to make sure she knew that I knew God personally and was sure about it.

That's exactly what you're doing for yourself. What my Mom saw in me you know about yourself. You know that your Christian upbringing hasn't made you a child of God. You didn't hide it. That's how the discussions on Kathy's good news started. Remember? And as I told you, I still am proud of you for not hiding the fact.

I'm forever thankful that my Mom didn't take chances about my personal relationship with God. I hope that "Kathy's good news" will lead you to be thankful to yourself for not taking those chances either.

You asked me to lead you to experience God the way I did. I thought of a way we can do it so it helps you build on your growing love for Jesus (see your e-mail dated 4/18/07).

Go back to the material on my personal experience of reconnection to God (attachment file to 4/22/07 e-mail). Read and re-read it. Jot down the steps that led me to the experience, and e-mail them to me. We'll take it from there, okay?

    Your friend,

    Doctor Wilson.

Date: 5/1/07

Subject: Kathy's good news

From: Kathy

To: Doctor Wilson

Dear Doctor,

    You want to know why I'm late in answering your e-mail? I'm saddened that your mom is dead. I lost a good friend before I knew her. And I'm mourning the loss. But she sounds so alive whenever I read the dialog between you and her. I'm so wrapped up in it I can't break free from it to work on it, if you see what I mean. So, please tell me if I did well on the exercise. Thanks.

Doctor Wilson's steps to reconnection to God:

One, you accepted that you were like all people. You desired to be let alone to do as you pleased. Two, you saw that this desire is rebellion against God. All evil acts come from it. Three, so you repented of that desire.

    Four, you believed that Jesus died so that you may not have to be separated forever from God because of that desire. Five, you asked God to forgive you and free you from the hold and dirt of that desire and its fruits, acts of sin.

Six, you believed that God did as you asked him. Seven, you believed that God entered your life and established a personal relationship with you right then. Eight, he changed you, and you knew it. Nine, you instantly felt some unusual peace and freedom. [And I guess some joy too, right?]

How did I do, Doctor?

Your friend,

Kathy.

Subject: Kathy's good news
Date: 5/5/07
From: Doctor Wilson
To: Kathy

Dear Kathy,

Excellent. I'm impressed by how well you did on the exercise. Now, Kathy, do this to further build on your growing love for Jesus. Retrieve the e-mail you've just sent me (the steps). Replace the word "you" in it with "I" or "me," as the case may be.

Read the rewritten e-mail aloud to yourself several times. It'll sound like you're talking to yourself about yourself. Listen and see if it also feels like you're taking those steps to be re-created by God. Send me a copy of the rewritten e-mail if you're convinced that you experienced its message. Don't forget to add any initial feelings you have in the process. Thanks.

Your friend,
Doctor Wilson.

Date: 5/10/07
Subject: Kathy's good news
From: Kathy
To: Doctor Wilson

Dear Doctor,

I did it, I did it, and I know it. I can't keep it down. Pat thinks I'm crazy.

At first it sounded funny hearing me talk to me about my-self. But as I read the rewritten e-mail over and over again it started feeling like I was actually taking the steps. And I did. I wish I were reading this to you face-to-face instead of writing you.

Kathy's steps to reconnection to God:

One, "I" accepted that "I was" like all people. "I" desired to be let alone to do as "I" pleased. Two, "I" saw that this desire is rebellion against God. All evil acts come from it. Three, so "I" repented of that desire.

Four, "I" believed that Jesus died so that "I" may not have to be separated forever from God because of that desire. Five, "I" asked God to forgive "me" and free "me" from the hold and dirt of that desire and its fruits, acts of sin. [I actually stopped and did it. Yes Doc, I did.]

Six, "I" believed that God did as "I" asked him. Seven, "I" believed that God has entered "my" life and established a personal relationship with "me" right then. Eight, he re-created "me" inside out. Nine, "I" instantly felt and am still feeling some deep joy, peace and freedom, I've never known.

Oh, Doctor, now I know I am a child of God. Yes, I do. Thank you.

> *Your friend,*
> *Kathy.*

Subject: Kathy's good news
Date: 5/10/07
From: Doctor Wilson
To: Kathy.

Happy Birth-day, Kathy!

Do you know that angels had a new-birth cele-bration for you right after you took those steps? Yes, they did. Listen, "There's joy before the angels of God over one sinner who repents," Jesus said (Luke 15:10, compare verse 7). So you see, there was a big celebration in heaven to mark your birth into the kingdom of God.

Hey, do you know that angels had a baby-birth-day celebration for Jesus on earth the night he was born in Bethlehem? "Glory to God in the highest," crowds of angels sang to shepherds watching their flock near-by that night. "And on earth, peace among [people] with whom he is pleased," (Luke 2:14 compare verses 8-13).

Now write down the date of your spiritual birth-day and remember to celebrate it yearly. Again, Kathy, Happy Birth-day! I'm rejoicing with you.

Your friend,
Doctor Wilson.

Subject: Kathy's good news
Date: 5/10/07
From: Doctor Wilson
To: Kathy

Hello Birth-day girl,
Here's something else you need to do immediately. Look back beyond the steps you took to enter a personal relationship with God. Look carefully over our earlier discussions. See if you can pull out the things that led you to the point when you took those steps. Let me know if you need help, okay?

You friend,
Doctor Wilson.

Date: 5/15/07
Subject: Kathy's good news
From: Kathy
To: Doctor Wilson

Dear Doctor,

I forgot to tell you. Wednesday, May 9, 2007 is my spiritual birthday. Please remember it and send me a card for my spiritual birthday, thanks.

But please tell me. Is this normal? Something terrible happened and I've lost some of my joy and peace, not all. I'm feeling bad for being rude to my sister. She did it first. Do you want the details? I guess I should just go ahead and tell you.

Sunday morning we were all getting ready for church. I went to my sister's room and asked her to zip me up. I turned my back to her to do it. She always does whenever I wear dresses with a long zip. She ignored me and went on packing her backpack and started walking away from me.

"Please, help me," I said and stood in front of her before she got to the doorway.

"Buy outfits you can manage; then you wouldn't have to depend on others to help you wear them," she said and shoved me aside.

"But you always ask me to help you," I said.

"Leave me alone. Dad has honked two times already in the driveway." She left me.

I changed into a different outfit and ran out to the car. The mood in the car said it all. I made us late to church (May 13, 2007).

At lunch after church, I pretended I didn't hear my sister when she asked me to pass the salt. I felt bad almost immediately. So I went to her room to ask forgiveness. She ignored me.

Today is three days and things haven't returned to normal between us. My sister doesn't return my smiles. I'm aching for her touch. What can I do, Doctor? Please help me.

Worried Kathy.

P/s I'll reply your latest e-mail later, thanks, Kathy.

Subject: Kathy's good news
Date: 5/17/07
From: Doctor Wilson
To: Kathy

Dear Kathy,

I'm sorry you're down. But know what, this sort of thing happens all the time. Feeling that bad about it is a sign that you're in relationship with God. It's conviction from the Holy Spirit. He convicts us anytime we do something wrong. It doesn't matter if others get us to do wrong. That's why you're feeling the way you feel.

I suggest that you write a letter to your sister and tell her how sorry you are. Tell her you miss her touch and smile and everything. And tell her you love her she's the only sister you have. And wait and see what she does. I'll be praying for you about that.

But always remember this, Kathy. Nothing we do wrong would ever disconnect us from God. Ephesians 2:4-6 (read it when you have time) says our recreation, reconnection, to God is as certain as Jesus' resurrection from death. Earlier in chapter 1:19-23, Paul said that the power that raised Jesus from death is the same power that recreated us and is working in us to make us into Jesus-likeness.

While we're on this, I think I should tell you something about temptation. Find in the attached file some guidelines on that. Always remember that temptations come to us all.

But the Holy Spirit who is with us doesn't only tell us we've done something wrong. No, he alerts us whenever temptations are about to hit. It's when we disregard his warnings and do the wrong thing that he convicts us to repent and get back in fellowship with God.

See how it all works out in the attached.

Your friend,

Doctor Wilson.

Attachment file to 5/16/07 e-mail

Temptation

Are temptations normal?

Yes, temptations are normal for believers in Jesus. Even Jesus was tempted (Luke 4:1-12 and Heb. 2:18, 4:15). To tempt, according to Webster's College Dictionary, is to induce, entice; to rouse desire in; be invited to, attract; to provoke, or run the risk of provoking.

Temptations seek to lure Christians to either do something they shouldn't do, or not do something they should. Temptations are hard to resist when we want that wrong thing we're being tempted to do, or when we feel right about it.

For example, someone wrongs us. We feel hurt, abused, or cheated. We could fight back in revenge. It feels right to do so. And we have opportunity to avenge ourselves. Everything within says, "You're a fool if you don't." Maybe friends are standing by saying, "You're going to let that jerk get away with what he or she has done to you?"

Momentarily, all that corners us. It appears we might lose the respect (and sometimes the friendship) of those cheering us on to fight back. What we do or don't do in times like that shows what kind of person we really are.

Christians who memorize scripture could recall the

appropriate one in the heat of temptation. "Do not be overcome by evil, but overcome evil with good," (Rom. 12:21) is a good one. But recalling the right scripture in the heat of temptation is one thing. Letting it calm us down to act right is another.

When do temptations come?

There's no set time, morning, evening, afternoon or night, for temptations to come. However, likely times are discernible. Since the main purpose of temptation is to entice or provoke Christians to hurt Jesus through disobedience, most of those temptations come at the time believers feel close to Jesus.

They have prayed a long time asking for something. And God has given it to them. Or, they didn't ask for it. But God gave it to them anyway. They feel singled out for God's favor. They're enjoying it. But often in that time of enjoyment, Christians tend to be less watchful. They let a false sense of 'I've reached it' take over.

They take their eyes off Jesus. Then wham. Temptation hits. Unaware, they make wrong choices or decisions. They choose wrong friends. Or, they give un-thought-out opinions on some social issues, etc.

Are Christians forgiven when they yield to temptation?

Yes. No sin, disobedience, or even rebellion of Christians is un-forgiven. Christians' past, present and future sins are all forgiven at the time they trusted God to save them. And he did. That's no license to sin and keep on sinning. No. Those who take that as a license show that they don't know what it is to be forgiven by grace. Because being forgiven by grace makes the forgiven forever thankful to God and forever careful not to abuse the grace of God.

They value their forgiveness. They do all they can to guard it. What's more, the Holy Spirit doesn't let them. He convicts them to repent whenever they sin. A guilt trip for sin often feels like conviction for sin. Here's the difference.

Convictions for sin always come from the Holy Spirit. When we repent, confess and leave the sin, we return to fellowship with God. Guilt trips don't behave like that. They lead to remorse, which is feeling sorry, not for why we did something wrong, not even for the wrong we've done, no.

Rather, we feel sorry because we're caught or that people have heard about it, and we obsess about the sin even after confession. Therefore doing damage control to save face becomes a preoccupation. In time, we'll sin those sins again no matter how hard we worked to save face. We never knew our sin or its root causes to repent of them.

The Bible calls the latter *worldly sorrow* for sin. It calls the former godly sorrow for sin. "For godly grief produces repentance that leads to salvation and brings no regret, but worldly grief produces death" (2 Cor. 7:10).

Where do temptations come from?

Luke 4:1-12 is a record of a time when Jesus was tempted. His tempter was Satan. That means some of our temptations come from Satan. In character, most of those kinds of temptations focus on luring us to turn our back on God after we've known him (become willful haters of God), compromise our faith, or abuse God's mercy.

But James 1:13-15 talks about another source of temptation. It's our desires.

> 13 Let no one say when he is tempted, "I'm tempted by God"; for God cannot be tempted with evil and he himself tempts no one; 14 but each person is tempted when he is lured and enticed by his own desire. 15 Then desire when it has conceived gives birth to sin; and sin when it is full-grown brings forth death (compare 1 John 2:15-17).

Other temptations come from among people we relate to on a daily basis. Jesus forewarned about the reality, "Woe to the world for temptations to sin! For it is necessary that temptations come, but woe to the man [person] by whom temptation comes!" (Matt. 18:7).

What's the difference between
"trials," and "temptations"?

Trials come from God. They test the genuineness and strength of our 'yes of faith' to God at a given time on a given issue. For example, God tested Abraham to sacrifice his son, Isaac, to God (Gen. 22:1-14). Then there was Mary, the mother of Jesus.

The Bible didn't specify that God tested her. But reading between the lines against her cultural background, we can see that God tested her "yes of faith" right after she'd given it. In Luke 1:26-38, we see Mary engaged to Joseph. They were betrothed, but their formal wedding might have been weeks or months away.

Then the angel of God came to her, saying, "There's a change of plans." By whom? "God wants you to carry the fetus of Messiah right away," the angel said.

"Sir, how can this be?" Mary said. "I'm a virgin engaged to be married." [Even if Mary didn't argue her case further in terms of her cultural setting, it ran through her mind].

Joseph might not believe her. He'd break the engagement. At once she'd become everyone's enemy. Her mom and dad wouldn't believe her either. They would be outraged for a bastard grandchild as well as the dowry Joseph's parents wouldn't return, since it was their daughter's infidelity that led Joseph to break the engagement. The priests would cry hell, fire, and brimstone and have her stoned.

In spite of all that, Mary gave a yes of faith to God when the angel told Mary that the Holy Spirit would oversee the planting of the fetus in her womb. Then Mary said, "I am the handmaid of the Lord; let it be to me according to your word" (Luke 1:38).

And the angel disappeared.

Luke's account swiftly moved to Mary's visit to Elizabeth (Luke 1:39-56). It was Matthew (1:18-25) who filled in the gap. Not surprisingly, Mary failed to convince Joseph that she was carrying the fetus of Messiah by the work of the Holy Spirit. Therefore he decided to break the engagement.

It was then that Mary went to visit her cousin Elizabeth, who was six months pregnant with John the Baptizer. As it was, Mary lost Joseph. She got ready to face the wrath of her mom and dad, the scorn of the community, and stoning at the command of the priests.

But unknown to her, God visited Joseph and confirmed Mary's message to him. In addition, God asked Joseph to take Mary back, marry her, and father the baby Jesus.

Indeed, God tested Mary on her 'yes of faith' to be the mother of Jesus. But like Abraham, she too passed the test. And just as Abraham got Isaac back, Mary also received Joseph back. Abraham became the father of all those who trust and depend on God to save them. And forever, the world will be grateful to Mary for mothering our Savior and Lord.

Trials test and strengthen us and our faith and trust

in God. Temptations, on the other hand, seek to turn us against God.

How do we overcome temptations?

Jesus taught that we should discern and deal with the ways in which we attract worldliness to ourselves, or get sucked into it.

> 8 So if your hand or foot causes you to sin, cut it off and throw it away. It is better to enter heaven crippled or lame than to be thrown into the unquenchable fire with both of your hands and feet. 9 And if your eye causes you to sin, [pluck] it out and throw it away. It is better to enter heaven [with one eye] than to have two eyes and be thrown into hell. (Matt. 18:8-9 LB compare 1 John 2:15-17)

Then Psalm 119:9-11 counsels. Hide God's word in your heart and you will not sin against him. Similarly, Galatians 5:1 urges us to value the freedom we have in Jesus. Then we'll do whatever it takes to guard it. In Ephesians 5:1, 7-10 we are to see ourselves as brand new and treat ourselves that way. We're children of light. Therefore we should live like that, doing only what's good, right, and true.

John 8:31-32 and 2 Peter 1:3-11 offer practical ways to focus on becoming more and more like Jesus and on growing in that commitment. The process is our resistance against temptations. Then we'll recall the right scripture and use it as a spiritual weapon in the heat of temptation.

When Jesus was tempted by Satan, three times, Jesus said: "It is written. That is, he quoted scripture to Satan'"" (Luke 4:4, 8, 10). And he set us example of how to defeat temptation.

Nothing in the Bible says temptations will not come to us, no. But everything there agrees that if we remain in Jesus, we will be more than conquerors, as he was. What comfort to know that Jesus was tempted in every way as we are. Yet he never sinned. Therefore he is able to keep us in our temptations (Heb. 2:18, 4:15 compare 1 Cor. 10:13).

Date: 5/18/07
Subject: Kathy's good news
From: Kathy
To: Doctor Wilson

Dear Doctor,
Thanks a lot for your advice. My sister and I are buddies again. We went shopping yesterday. She even bought me a dress with a long zip at the back. Can you believe that? She knows I like dresses with long zips. We had lots of fun.
Doctor, I like the document on temptation a lot. I like the questions you asked and answered. You've given me something to go back to again and again. It'll help me stay out of trouble.
I like the difference you made between convictions and guilt

trips. The difference between trials and temptations is also helpful.

I find your story on Mary very interesting. I didn't know she went through all that trouble to be the mother of Jesus. My folder for Kathy's good news is growing fat with goodies. Thanks, Doctor.

I'm still working on the assignment on the things that led me to the point when I took those steps to enter a personal relationship with God. I'll be done soon.

Your friend,
Kathy.

Subject: Kathy's good news
Date: 5/20/07
From: Doctor Wilson
To: Kathy

Dear Kathy,

I'm glad the relationship between you and your sister has returned to normal. I prayed it did. I'm also glad that you find the document on temptation helpful.

But I'm sorry I didn't give you much help with the assignment. Now go dig, dig, and dig into what we called "background stuff." All the answers are there. And know what? Take your time with it, okay?

Your friend,

Doctor Wilson.

Date: 5/30/07
Subject: Kathy's good news
From: Kathy
To: Doctor Wilson

Dear Doctor,

This assignment took so long because it was hard. But I'm glad I did it. It helped me see a lot more in the background stuff. Thanks for asking me to do it. Please, tell me how well I did. Thanks.

The things that led me to the steps

One, new understanding of lostness: Now I know there are people who are lost and don't know it. And there are others like me who are lost and know it. I knew I was lost but I didn't have a word for it. Now I know I was a false start. I knew Christianity and tried to live like a Christian without a personal relationship with God. Thanks, Doctor. I escaped becoming a 'willful hater of God' in adulthood.

Two, new understanding of the origin of lostness: Now I know that Satan invented sin. Therefore he owned the power of sin and death. Eve and Adam's rebellion put us (their descendants) under that power.

Three, new understanding of sin: Now I know that the desire to be let alone to do as one pleases is the mother of all sins. Therefore it's not enough to repent of our sins. We must also repent of that desire.

Four, new understanding of Jesus and his love for us: Jesus provided reconnection to God. And he himself is the reconnection. He's the good news. He met and defeated Satan and the power of sin and death. That is great.

But this is what makes me weep anytime I remember it. You said, "Jesus, the sinless one, made himself sin in his crucifixion, and God the Father punished him as sin deserves." I can never forget that. I wonder if I can ever love Jesus enough in return.

Five, examples of people Jesus changed: This was the first time I saw the Samaritan woman, Mary Magdalene, Zacchaeus, and the legion demoniac as people Jesus led one-on-one into a personal relationship with God. For the first time their stories came alive to me as examples of conversion.

But you and your mom are something else. Your mom didn't take it that the Christian upbringing she and your dad gave you necessarily made you a child of God. She took steps to be sure you entered a personal relationship with God, and that you knew it, and were sure about it. I can never forget that. I wish all Christian parents would do that for their kids.

And you, you took the steps your mom taught you. And you entered a personal relationship with God when you were ten. Seven months later you led your dad, a churchgoer, to enter a personal relationship with God. And though your dad died three days later, you didn't become bitter. You became an instant evangelist instead. And you're still at it.

Thanks to your mom and you. You were the first people I met who showed me that Jesus makes a difference in people today.

But know what? There's one more thing. Six, the Holy Spirit: It was the Holy Spirit who opened my mind to see all those new things in Bible stories I've heard over and over again in Sunday school. Don't you agree? It was he who got me to talk to you at the end of your talks in our church. He was the one who led me to fall in love with Jesus. It was the Holy Spirit who helped me to hear and see myself in the exercise on the steps that led me into a personal relationship with God.

Now I know that I'm a child of God. Nothing, nothing, can change that. No.

How did I do, Doctor?

Your friend,

Kathy.

Subject: Kathy's good news
Date: 6/2/07
From: Doctor Wilson
To: Kathy.

Dear Kathy,

No, a million times no. Nothing can take from you the experience of entering a personal relationship with God. Remember, your mind and will were involved in taking the steps to the experience. And nothing can separate you from the love of Jesus either (read it in Rom. 8:31-39). You know why? It's the work of the Holy Spirit.

Now to the assignment. As usual, Kathy, you did excellently. Bravo. Let's make a capsule of the things that you've listed as background to the steps that you took to enter a personal relationship with God. We'll make sure to lose nothing while we shrink them.

Below, I cut and paste what you'd listed in your e-mail. I'll tag appropriate labels to the 'cut and paste.' The labels become the recipe for the capsule. I'm excited. Are you?

The things that led me [Kathy] to the steps *(copied from your e-mail dated 5/30/07).*

One, new understanding of lostness: Now I know there are people who are lost and don't know it. And there are others like me who are lost and know it. I knew I was lost but I didn't have a word for it. Now I know I was a false start. I knew Christianity and tried to live like a Christian without a personal relationship with God. Thanks to you, Doctor, I escaped becoming a 'willful hater of God' in adulthood.

(the scriptures)

Two, new understanding of the origin of lostness: Now I know that Satan invented sin. Therefore he owned the power of sin and death. Eve and Adam's rebellion put us all (their descendants) under that power.

(the scriptures)

Three, new understanding of sin: Now I know that the desire to be let alone to do as one pleases is the mother of all sins. Therefore it's not enough to repent of our sins. We must also repent of that desire.

(the scriptures)

Four, new understanding of Jesus and his love for us: Jesus is not only the provider of reconnection to God. He is the reconnection. He's the good news. He met and defeated Satan and the power of sin and death. That is great.

But you know what draws tears to my eyes anytime I remember it? You said, "Jesus, the sinless one, made himself sin, and God the Father punished him as sin deserves." I can never forget that. I wonder if I can ever love Jesus enough in return?

(Jesus)

Five, examples of people Jesus changed: This was the first time I saw the Samaritan woman, Mary Magdalene, Zacchaeus, and the legion demoniac as people Jesus led one-on-one into a personal relationship with God. For the first time their stories came alive to me as examples of conversion.

But you and your mom are something else. Your mom didn't take it that the Christian upbringing she and your dad gave you necessarily made you a child of God. She took steps to be sure you entered a personal relationship with God, and that you knew it, and were sure about it. I can never forget that. I wish all Christian parents do that for their kids.

And you, you took the steps she showed you. And you

entered a personal relationship with God when you were ten. Seven months later you led your dad, a churchgoer, to enter a personal relationship with God. And though your dad died three days later, you didn't become bitter. You became an instant evangelist instead. And you're still at it.

Thanks to your mom and you. You were the first people I met who showed me that Jesus makes a difference in people today.

(people)

But know what? There's one more thing. Six, the Holy Spirit: It was the Holy Spirit who opened my mind to see all those new things in old Bible stories I've heard over and over again in Sunday school. Don't you agree? It was he who got me to talk to you when you came to our church. He was the one who led me to fall in love with Jesus. It was the Holy Spirit who helped me to hear and see myself in the exercise on the steps that led me into a personal relationship with God.

(the Holy Spirit)

Pulled together, we have

- the Holy Spirit
- people
- Jesus, and
- the scriptures.

  One thing is missing. What is it? It's
- trust

See below a cut and paste from your e-mail on "the steps," dated 5/10/07. In that section you used the word "believe:"

Four, **"I"** *believed that Jesus died so that "I" may not have to be separated forever from God because of that desire [the desire to be let alone to do as "I" please]. Five, "I" asked God to forgive "me" and free "me" from the hold and dirt of that desire and its fruits, acts of sin. [I actually stopped and did it. Yes Doc, I did.]*

Six, **"I"** *believed that God did as "I" asked him. Seven,* **"I"** *believed that God has entered "my" life and established a personal relationship with "me" right then. Eight, he re-created "me" inside out.*

Believing that led you to be re-created wasn't mind acceptance of the facts. You've had the head knowledge all along. But it didn't lead you into a personal relationship with God. No. What made the difference this time around was **"trust."** In a way, **trust** bridged the gap between head knowledge and heart experience.

Here then are all the ingredients of the capsule:

- **the Holy Spirit** (his presence and activity)
- **people** (visibly changed people)
- **Jesus** (as provider of re-connection to God, and as the reconnection; [you began

to love him dearly since you realized that])

- **the scriptures** (new understanding of the scriptures)
- **trust** (willingness to surrender love of control to God, and willingness to receive the gift of forgiveness, life, and the Holy Spirit from God).

All of them acted together, not in isolation.

That was how you experienced the good news. Now read the attached file, titled, 'The good news according to Jesus.' Take special note of the capsule of his statement of the good news.

Then read the e-mail that immediately follows. In it, I compare the capsule of your experience of the good news to the capsule of the good news according to Jesus. Tell me how the parallel hits you.

Your friend,

Doctor Wilson.

Attachment file to 6/2/07 e-mail

The good news according to Jesus

Luke 24:36-53,

36 As they were saying this, Jesus himself stood among

them. 37 But they were startled and frightened, and supposed that they saw a spirit. 38 And he said to them, "Why are you troubled, and why do questionings rise in your hearts? 39 See my hands and my feet, that it is I myself; handle me, and see; for a spirit has not flesh and bones as you see that I have." 41 And while they still disbelieved for joy, and wondered, he said to them, "have you anything here to eat?" 42 They gave him a piece of broiled fish, 43 and he took it and ate before them.

44 Then he said to them, "These are my words which I spoke to you while I was still with you, that everything written about me in the law of Moses and the prophets and the psalms must be fulfilled." 45 Then he opened their minds to understand the scriptures, 46 and said to them, "Thus it is written that the Christ should suffer and on the third day rise from the dead, 47 and that repentance and forgiveness of sins should be preached in his name to all nations, beginning from Jerusalem. 48 You are witnesses of these things, 49 And behold, I send the promise of my father upon you; but stay in the city, until you are clothed with power from on high."

50 Then he led them out as far as Bethany, and lifting up his hands he blessed them. 51 While he blessed them, he parted from them, and was carried up into heaven. 52 And they returned to Jerusalem with great joy, 53 and were continually in the temple blessing God.

Summary

Verses 36-43, the commissioner of the good news
- the bodily resurrected Jesus (verses 36-43)

Verses 44-45, the source of the good news
- all the scriptures (verse 44)
- disentangled understanding of all the scriptures (verse 45)

Verses 46-47, the theme of the good news
- the crucified and bodily resurrected Jesus according to the scriptures (verse 46)
- repentance and forgiveness in the name of Jesus to be preached to all nations (verse 47)

Verses 48-49, witnesses of the good news
- credible witnesses (verse 48)
- clothed witnesses (verse 49)

Verses 50-53, the fragrance of the good news
- being blessed to be a blessing (verses 50-51)
- being joyful, prayerful and praiseful (verses 52-53).

Capsulated

According to Jesus, the factors that work together in the good news, making it the good news, are

- **visibly changed people** (they're credible and Holy Spirit-filled, and joyful, prayerful and praiseful, verses 48-53)
- **the Holy Spirit** (he empowers the witnesses to reflect Jesus; he also helps them and their hearers to understand the scriptures, verses 45 and 49)
- **the scriptures** (they predicted Jesus' coming and what he'd do; and they recorded that he'd come and done as predicted; they call for repentance, and offer forgiveness, in Jesus' name, verses 44-47)
- **Jesus** (the resurrected and enthroned Jesus as commissioner of the good news, and Jesus himself as the good news, verses 36-43 and 46-47).

Jesus stated the good news with built-in-reality check. The built-in-reality check is made up of seeing the good news, hearing the good news, and experiencing the good news all at once. That's possible only when people who are visibly changed by the good news tell it. Their visibly changed lives make them credible and authentic.

Visible Jesus-likeness in them also shows that they're Spirit-filled. In evidence, the Spirit is right there to confirm their credibility and the truth of their message about Jesus. It too is consistent with Jesus as revealed in all the scriptures.

As Creator of people (John 1:1-5, Col. 1:15-20), Jesus knows a lot about people. He knows that things people see, hear, and experience impact them. But they quickly forget the things they only hear. Or they file them away as head knowledge. Certainly, Jesus didn't want the good news to be something people file away as head knowledge, or easily forgotten.

No. He wanted the good news to change people inside out as they hear it. Therefore he stated it with the life-changing built-in-reality check. That's the wisdom in Jesus' statement of the good news.

Subject: Kathy's good news
Date: 6/2/07
From: Doctor Wilson
To Kathy

Dear Kathy,

Did you realize that you experienced the good news in exactly the way Jesus wants it to be experienced?

You experienced the reality-check Jesus built into his statement of the good news. At the same time, you saw, heard, and experienced the changes that the good news promises to make in people. Right there and then you stopped imagining how it works and what it looks like. At once you entered a personal relationship with God.

The parallel between your experience and Jesus' built-in-reality check makes the good news according to Jesus Kathy's good news. What do you say, Kathy?

Your friend,
Doctor Wilson.

Date: 6/14/07
Subject: Kathy's good news
From: Kathy
To: Doctor Wilson

Doctor, I agree, and I'm surprised. Thanks. But know what? I experienced the good news when you weren't actually presenting it to me. I guess that was the work of the Holy Spirit. He must have used the likeness of Jesus I saw in your mom and in you, and my new understanding of the scriptures and of Jesus to give me the experience.

This wasn't the case in the past. That's why I wasn't getting the good news. My search is over. Now I know I've got the good news. Thanks a lot for guiding me.

Now, Doctor, I have good news for you. I'm still recovering from the shock of it. Before your e-mail and the attachment on the good news according to Jesus came, I was on the computer reading my e-mail to you on the things that led me to the steps (it's dated 5/30/07). Daddy came in to kiss me good night.

"What are you reading this late, sweetheart?" he said.

Before I knew it he stood behind me reading the document over my head. "Who's Doctor?" he asked, massaging my neck and shoulders. I told him. He sat at the edge of my bed and said. "You're writing this to him?"

"Yes, Daddy."

"Scroll down."

I did and he read all of it. Then he said, "What's all that about?"

I told him the story of Kathy's good news.

"How long have you and the Doctor been writing each other on this?"

"Since March, 2007."

"Are you kidding?"

"No, Daddy."

He asked me to copy him the 5/30/07 e-mail he met me reading, and the one on the steps I took to enter a personal relationship with God. [It's Kathy's steps to reconnection (5/10/07).] Then he kissed me good night and went out. I copied them to him immediately. Before I went to bed, I prayed, 'Lord, please keep Daddy from getting angry about this.'

At breakfast he said, "Kathy, I'm proud of you."

I thought, he must have read what I copied him before he went to bed last night. Now what? He looked at me and said, "Get ready, Kathy, to read the two documents to the family after dinner tonight."

My heart missed a beat. And I nearly fell off the chair.

"What documents?" Mom said. She and my brother and sister looked at Daddy and me wanting to know. It was good Daddy spoke because I was too scared to say anything.

"Patient, honey. You'll know," Daddy said, and turned to me half smiling. "I'll make copies for everyone."

After we'd cleared the dinner table Daddy told the history of Kathy's good news. "These are pieces from e-mail correspondence between Kathy and her mentor, the Doctor, on that," Daddy said while he gave out the copies. Then he said, "Kathy, you're on, read to us."

See in the attached file copies of the two e-mails I read. Mom was first to speak after I finished reading.

"I'm ashamed of myself," she said looking down. "But, I'm proud of you, Kathy. From this moment," she looked at me, "I'm no longer a false start. Thank you, Kathy. Thank you." Tears dropped from her eyes.

"Me too," my sister said and wiped tears with both hands. She leaned over and hugged me on the side.

"Good words, Kathy," my brother said. And he gave me a paper napkin across the table to wipe my eyes and nose. "I'm proud of you," he said.

Daddy got up and came to me. He kissed me on the head and said, "Sweetheart, thank you, thank you. We're all proud of you," his voice broke.

What do you call this, Doctor? I'm still in shock.

Your friend,

Kathy.

Subject: Kathy's good news
Date: 6/14/07
From: Doctor Wilson
To: Kathy

Dear Kathy,

Congratulations. Again I say, congratulations. You entered a personal relationship with God on

Wednesday, 5/9/07. A little over a month later, you led your mom and sister to do the same. That's great. Remember Luke 15:10? There was a new-birth celebration in heaven for them also. Kathy, I'm proud of you.

I found in the document you attached the two e-mails you read to the family: The one is "The things that led me [Kathy] to the steps" (in 5/30/07 e-mail), and the other is "Kathy's steps to reconnection to God" (in 5/10/07 e-mail).

I took the liberty to put them in one document. I hope you don't mind? I also tweaked them a little to include the scenes at the dinner table. And I named the combined document "The good news according to Kathy." Find it in the attached file. Take a look at it and tell me what you think. Thanks.

Your friend,

Doctor Wilson.

Attachment file to 6/14/07 e-mail

The Good News According to Kathy

After the family dinner, Daddy told the history (he'd learned from me) about 'Kathy's good news.' "These are pieces from e-mail correspondence between Kathy and her mentor the Doctor on 'Kathy's good news'," Daddy said while giving out the copies he'd made. Then he turned to me and said, "Kathy, you're on, read to us."

I have finally entered a personal relationship with God. And I know it. Yes, I do. These are the things that led me to the steps I took to enter the relationship.

The things that led me to the steps

One, a new understanding of the scriptures:
a) I now know there are people who are lost and don't know it. And there are others like me who are lost and know it (Luke 15:1-24). I knew I was lost but I didn't have a word for it. Now I know I was a false start.

I knew Christianity and tried to live like a Christian. But I didn't have a personal relationship with God. Thanks to the Doctor, I escaped becoming a 'willful hater of God' in adulthood when my childhood experience of church would become meaningless to me.

b) I now know that Satan invented sin (Isaiah 14:12-21, Hebrews 2:14-18). Therefore he owned the power of sin and death. Eve and Adam's rebellion against God put us (their descendants) under that power (Gen. 3, Rom. 5).

c) I now know that the desire to be let alone to do as one pleases is the mother of all sins (Isa. 53:6 compare Gen. 3). Therefore it's not enough to repent of our sins. We must also repent of that desire (1 John 1:1-10).

Two, a new understanding of Jesus and his love for us: Jesus provided reconnection to God. And he himself is the reconnection. He's the good news, because he met and defeated Satan and the power of sin and death. That is great (Isa. 53, 61:1-2, Heb. 2:14-18).

But what often makes me weep is a statement the Doctor made. He said, "Jesus, the sinless one, made himself sin, and God the Father punished him as sin deserves," (2 Cor. 5:21, 8:9). I can never forget that. I wonder if I can ever love Jesus enough in return.

Three, visibly changed people:
I saw new light in examples of people Jesus changed. For the first time I saw the Samaritan woman, Mary Magdalene, Zacchaeus, and the legion demoniac as people Jesus led one-on-one into a personal relationship with God. For the first time their stories came alive to me as examples of conversion (Mark 5:1-20, Luke 8:1-3, Luke 19:1-10, John 4:1-42, John 20:1-18).

But the Doctor and his mom are something else. His mom didn't take it for granted that the Christian upbringing she and his dad gave him necessarily made him a child of God. She took steps to be sure he entered a personal relationship with God, and that he knew it, and he was sure about it. I can never forget that. I wish all Christian parents would do that for their kids.

And the Doctor, he took the steps his mom taught him. And he entered a personal relationship with God when he was ten. Seven months later he led his dad, a churchgoer, to enter a personal relationship with God. Then his dad died three days later. But he didn't become bitter. He became an instant evangelist instead. And he's still at it.

Thanks to the Doctor and his mom. They were the first people whose lives showed me that Jesus makes a difference in people today.

But, there's one more thing.

Four, new understanding of the work and experience of the Holy Spirit:
It was the Holy Spirit who opened my mind to see all those new things in Bible stories I've heard over and over again in Sunday school. It was he who got me to talk to the Doctor at the end of his series of talks in our church. The Holy Spirit was the one who led me to fall in love with Jesus. It was the Holy Spirit who helped me to hear and see myself in the exercise on the steps that led me into a personal relationship with God.

Now I know that I'm a child of God. Nothing, nothing, can change that. No.

Those things led me to the following steps I took to enter a personal relationship with God.

Kathy's steps to reconnection to God:

One, I accepted that I was like all people. I desired to be let alone to do as I please. Two, I saw that that desire is rebellion against God. All evil acts come from it. Three, so "I" repented of that desire.

Four, I believed with all my heart that Jesus died so that I may not have to be separated forever from God because of that desire. Five, I asked God to forgive me and free me from the hold and dirt of that desire and its fruits, acts of sin.

Six, I believed that God did as I asked him. Seven, I believed that God has entered my life and established a personal relationship with me right then. Eight, he re-created me inside out. Nine, I instantly felt and am still feeling joy, peace, and freedom, I've never known.

Now I know I am a child of God. Yes, I do. Thank you to the Doctor, my mentor.

Mom was first to speak after I'd finished reading. "I'm ashamed of myself," she said looking down. "But I'm proud of you, Kathy. From this moment," she looked at me, "I'm no longer a false start. Thank you, Kathy, thank you." Tears dropped from her eyes.

"Me too," my sister said and wiped tears with both hands. She leaned over and hugged me on the side.

"Good words," my brother said. And he gave me a paper napkin across the table to wipe my eyes and nose. "I'm proud of you."

Daddy got up and came to me. He kissed me on the head and said, "Sweetheart, thank you, thank you. We're all proud of you," his voice broke.

Date: 6/16/07
Subject: Kathy's good news
From: Kathy
To: Doctor Wilson

Dear Doctor,
I like "The good news according to Kathy," very much. Seeing it all together in that form makes me weep again. Thanks a lot. I think I'll ask Daddy to show it to the editors of the church's quarterly magazine. Who knows, they might put it in the kids' column. I'll tell you if they do.
Your friend,
Kathy.

Subject: Kathy's good news
Date: 6/18/07
From: Doctor Wilson
To: Kathy

Yes, yes, Kathy,
How exciting if the church magazine published "The good news according to Kathy." It'd be your conversion story and witness in print. And I'd like a clipping for keeps.

Now, Kathy, find in the attached file some guide-lines on the quiet-time. But here I share with you a quiet-time I did recently. The passage I read was

Colossians 3:12-17 (NIV).

12 Therefore, as God's chosen people, holy and beloved, clothe yourselves with compassion, kindness, humility, gentleness and patience. 13 Bear with each other and forgive whatever grievances you may have against one another. Forgive as the Lord forgave you. 14 And over all these virtues put on love, which binds them all together in perfect unity.

15 Let the peace of Christ rule in your hearts, since as members of the one body you were called to peace. And be thankful. 16 Let the word of Christ dwell in you richly as you teach and admonish one another with all wisdom and as you sing psalms, hymns and spiritual songs with gratitude in your hearts to God. 17 And whatever you do, whether in word or deed, do it all in the name of the Lord Jesus, giving thanks to God the Father through him.

After the first reading I wrote in my journal:

'Being at peace with others and ourselves will result (verse 15) when we have Jesus-like qualities in us (verses 12-14). The end of verse 15, and verses 16-17, demand that we do everything in Jesus' name, and that we be thankful to God through Jesus.'

I read the passage again with those thoughts in

mind. Then I saw that verse 17 lent itself to memorization. So I memorized it at once. Verse 16 said that when Jesus' word takes root in us, it'll make us fruitful.

So I asked, "How would Jesus' word sink roots in us?"

And I answered, "through meditation and memorization and understanding and obedience."

"Yes, but how exactly?"

I was lost at this point. So I prayed, "Lord, please help."

When I returned to the passage to read it again, I saw that there was too much in it for one devotion time. For the present time, then, I'd focus on verses 12-14. Later, I would concentrate on verses 15-17. At once I saw verse 16 as gateway to understanding both parts (verses 12-14 and verses 15-17).

In a word, verse 16 says we let Jesus' word sink in. To let verses 12-14 (my focus for the day) sink in, I decided, first, to remove all the "fat" from Jesus-like traits listed there. And I got compassion, kindness, humility, gentleness, and patience, [to] bear with, [to] forgive, and love. That's a mixture of verbs and nouns.

So, second, I decided to convert the nouns and verbs into adjectives. The conversion gave me, compassionate, kind, humble, gentle, patient, forbearing, forgiving, and loving. Third, I grouped the one-word Jesus-like characteristics for easy memorization like this:

- compassionate, and kind
- humble, gentle, and patient
- forbearing, forgiving, and loving.

The process gave me a capsule of some characteristics of Jesus. It also made them easy to memorize and recall. I prayed the capsule as my desire, asking God to help me to be like that.

Guess how long all that took me. Twenty minutes. I spent another minute jotting down a reminder that I have the rest of the passage (verse 15-17) to cover in my next time with God (the quiet time).

Okay, Kathy, have a great week.

Your friend,

Doctor Wilson.

P.s. Kathy, look out for samples of monthly devotional guides I've mailed to you by US-mail. Read the stuff on the guidelines on the quiet time before you start using them. Doctor Wilson.

Attachment file to 6/18/07 e-mail

Some Guidelines for the Quiet Time

When Ephraim told me this story years ago, he didn't say

the name of the person or the place of the story. But I like the story. It highlights the need to use a step-by-step plan in reading the Bible. So I take the freedom to call the person in the story, Brad.

Brad grew up in a Christian home. But his home wasn't really, really Christian. Typically, his mom and dad cursed and quarreled on the way to and from church. Brad and his sister, four years younger, dared not cough in the back seat. Or they'd be sucked into the raging flames.

Brad reached break point at age 15 and he decided to run away from home. A perfect time to sneak out was Sunday afternoon while his mom and dad napped. He picked up the family Bible from the dining table and took it to his room to seek one last word from God.

He set the Bible on his lap, closed his eyes and said, "I'll flip the Bible open and thrust my finger on the pages. The verse on which my finger rests will be God's counsel to me." Then the counted down, five, four, three, two, one, and he flipped the Bible open.

He thrust the finger in as planned. When he opened his eyes he found his finger resting on Matthew 27:5. It said, "And he went and hung himself."

"No," Brad said. "That was Judas Iscariot after he'd regretted betraying Jesus to the Pharisees. God wouldn't ask me to go hang myself, no way."

So he closed his eyes and did it a second time. When he opened his eyes, he found his finger resting on Luke 10:37. It read, "Go and do likewise."

"No way," Brad said. "This is not correct."

A third time, he did as he'd done before. The verse his finger rested on this time read, "Go do quickly what you have to do" (John 13:27).

Brad was a smart kid. He got the message. It said, "Go commit suicide right now." That wasn't what he wanted. So he tossed the Bible to the floor. He slouched in the chair and said, "Rubbish, rubbish, rubbish…."

The quiet time offers a better way to read the Bible. "Quiet" means being quiet. Keen quiet time observers find a place and time when they can be quiet. They treat the quiet-time as time alone with God. They have handy

- a Bible (they can read and understand)
- a devotional guide, and
- a pen and notebook.

The weekly or monthly devotional guide gives the day's text. [Some devotional guides print out the selected passage of the Bible at the top of the page.] Eager quiet-time observers read the text two or three times. Then they meditate on thoughts that jump out at them while reading.

They jot down those thoughts before reading the commentary on the passage in the devotional guide. To those thoughts they add insights they pick up from the commentary. They end the quiet-time by converting what they learn into prayer. The process gives them a thought they carry with them throughout the day.

Starting to observe the quiet-time may be difficult because it demands self-discipline. But with time, the habit sticks. It becomes joyful and meaningful. Serious observers don't get boringly addicted to the quiet-time, no. Rather, they go to it eagerly. They look forward to

- hear God talk to them through his word, the Bible, and
- talk to God in prayer after they've heard him.

Churches and Christian bookstores carry lots of devotional guides. The ones that have a Bible verse and a page long commentary on it for daily reading tend to favor on-the-run time with God. Not so the ones that assign a passage of scripture for daily reading. By encouraging readers to read the passage from the Bible itself, they eliminate the fast-food attitude toward the quiet-time. They help readers to slow down and treat their time with God with respect.

The latter devotional guides also ask leading questions to help readers search the scriptures further for themselves. The following are some website links for those types of devotional guides:

http://scriptureunion.gospelcom.net (Scripture Union)
http://www.ivpress.com (InterVarsity Press)
http://www.walkthru.org (Navigators)

Date: 6/24/07
Subject: Kathy's good news
From: Kathy
To: Doctor Wilson

Dear Doctor,

Thanks a lot for the stuff on the quiet time. Brad's story is funny but serious. I wonder. Why would people treat the Bible like magic? Perhaps they don't know any better. I know I'll like the copies of the devotional guides you've sent me. I'll tell you as soon as I receive them and start using them.

But Doctor, I have sad news. I've lost my friend Pat. She didn't die. No. Did I tell you we go to the same school? She came to the school because of her uncle, her dad's younger brother. He goes to our church. And two of his kids go to our school. Pat came to church on and off. Her parents and her sister don't go to church. I told you they practice the occult. Remember? [See e-mail dated 4/6/07]

Today at church I bumped into Frank, Pat's cousin. He's two years older than Pat and me. I asked him about Pat.

"Didn't she tell you?" he said. "Oh yeah, she couldn't. She's forbidden to talk to you. The family is gone on a trip to France."

I was shocked to hear 'Forbidden to talk to you.' Me? But that was the beginning. What Frank said next, did it.

"Pat's mom and dad are pulling her out of our school."

"Why?" I asked.

"Her mom said you're a bad influence on her. Dad said we

shouldn't tell you."

"Me, how?" I said and started crying.

"Excuse me," Frank said and walked away.

I've wept all day. I couldn't eat lunch. Daddy and Mom said I should let it go. But it's hard. Pat is my best friend. Do you have any word of advice for me, Doctor?

Your troubled friend,

Kathy.

Subject: Kathy's good news
Date: 6/24/07
From: Doctor Wilson
To: Kathy.

Dear Kathy,

How sad to lose a close friend. Particularly when you weren't given a chance to put closure on the friendship. I'm so sorry, Kathy. Give yourself a bit of time to learn to get over it.

Meanwhile, look at it this way. Pat's mom accused you of being bad influence on Pat. What's that supposed to mean?

The only influence I can think of is your untiring search for a personal relationship with God. Or am I mistaken? If that is the case, and I think it is, then see this whole thing as persecution.

Let's put it all in context, shall we? You entered a

personal relationship with God a little over a month ago. Within the same period, your testimony led your mom and sister, churchgoers, to do the same. All that gladdened God and rocked heaven with joy (Luke 15:10).

But that also outraged Satan and his kingdom. They didn't only lose a twelve-year-old, you, to Jesus. Through you two other victims of false start, your mom and sister, are freed from the trap. They've also gone to Jesus. Why wouldn't Satan and his kingdom fight back? The fight-back takes many forms. Whatever the form, Kathy, it is persecution. But often it's people's dislike for God's interference in their lives that bridges Satan's hatred for Jesus to keen followers of Jesus.

So, you're suffering persecution for the sake of Jesus. Now, listen to what Jesus, Paul and Peter said about it out of experience.

Jesus: Blessed are those who are persecuted for righteousness sake, for theirs is the kingdom of heaven. Blessed are you when men [people] revile you and persecute you and utter all kinds of evil against you falsely on my account. Rejoice and be glad, for your reward is great in heaven, for so men [people] persecuted the prophets who were before you (Matt. 5:10-12).

Paul: Indeed all who desire to live a godly life in Christ will be persecuted (2 Tim. 3:14).

Peter: If you are reproached for the name of Christ, you are blessed, because the Spirit of glory and of God rests upon you (1 Pet. 4:14).

So you see, persecutions for the sake of righteousness are a sign that we're in step with God. Therefore in your heart, Kathy, try and forgive Pat's mom and dad. Forgive Pat too. Remember, Pat is like you. She's a minor. She can't go against her parents' word and get away with it.

But again in your heart, continue to love Pat. Pray for her (I'll be praying with you on that). Let's ask God to show himself to her by any means. And he will. Give me five days and I'll send you a document on Reckless Love. Do you know it's the most powerful thing for handling this sort of thing?

Okay, friend, cheer up.

Love,

Doctor Wilson.

Date: 6/24/07
Subject: Kathy's good news
From: Kathy
To: Doctor Wilson.

Oh Doctor, thank you, thank you, thank you. It feels like I'm floating, weightless on my feet. Your words freed me and healed me. I'm happy again. Daddy and Mom and my brother and sister will be glad to see me this happy. Mom may even allow me a snack before dinner because I was so heartbroken I couldn't eat lunch. Thanks a lot, Doctor.

I can't wait for the document on Reckless Love. The title is exciting.

Your friend,

Kathy.

Subject: Kathy's good news

Date: 6/30/07

From: Doctor Wilson

To: Kathy

Dear Kathy,

I'm glad my counsel helped you. Find attached the document I promised on Reckless Love. As I said, its message is the most powerful thing on earth. Hurry.

Your friend,

Doctor Wilson.

Attachment file for 6/30/07 e-mail

Reckless Love

Jesus, God in human form, started a revolution of love on

earth. It was so strong it turned a God-defiant environment characterized by divisions, hate, and violence--fear, force, and fighting, upside down. How could a revolution dressed in weakness, humility and servanthood do that?

Everywhere, messengers of the revolution oozed love. That angered oppressive powers. Outraged political, religious and social leaders tried to crash the revolution through torture and murder. They couldn't. The more they tortured the revolution, the more it spread. Enemies of the revolution of love nicknamed the revolution's messengers, people-of-love and concluded, "This is what being with Jesus does to people."

The enemies were right. Jesus was the only one who loved priests and prostitutes, theologians and tax collectors, the powerful and powerless, the rich and poor, and his friends and enemies, alike. He died for them all.

Like Jesus, his followers were nobodies by social standards. But the following character traits distinguished them. First, they never tired of doing good to people, good people and bad people alike (Gal. 6:9-10).

Second, they unconditionally accepted and cared for one another irrespective of their backgrounds (John 13:34-35). Not only that, third, they loved and prayed for people who treated them like dirt (Matt. 5:43-48). Fourth, they wholeheartedly loved God (Mark 12:30). Nothing was too dear to give up for him.

Paul calls that reckless love in action (1 Cor. 13:4-8). It's reckless because it's patient and kind when stressed out. That's because it's not proud, rude, self-seeking, or easily angered. Therefore it's at peace with itself, others and God. It doesn't envy, boast, keep a record of wrongs, or rejoice when bad things happen to enemies. And it doesn't give up. No.

Rather, it always rejoices when the truth wins out. It always protects, trusts, hopes, and perseveres. Isn't that outrageous? It is, because reckless love is God's outrageous love in people. "The fruit of the Spirit," Galatians 5:22-23 says, "is love, joy, peace, and patience; kindness, goodness, faithfulness, gentleness, and self-control."

God's outrageous love is sufficient, selfless, and sacrificial. When reckless love takes after its parent, outrageous love, it too becomes sufficient, selfless, and sacrificial. Jesus said, referring to himself, there's no greater love than this, "that a man [person] lay down his life for his friends," (John 15:13).

Jesus' friends included Peter, Zacchaeus, Mary Magdalene, and the Samaritan woman. He wished Caiaphas, the Pharisees, Herod, Pilate, and the Roman soldiers who denied him justice, mocked him, and crucified him were among them. So he prayed for them just before he died, "Father, forgive them; for they know not what they do" (Luke 23:34).

Reckless love does no less. As a true child of outrageous love, reckless love could only show the family likeness. Jesus insists that it is that family likeness, love in expression, that will convince the world that

- God sent Jesus to inaugurate a revolution of reckless love on earth, and
- God did it out of outrageous love for people on earth (John 17:20-23).

Date: 7/1/07
Subject: Kathy's good news
From: Kathy
To: Doctor Wilson

Dear Doctor,

I can't stop reading the document on reckless love. I've never thought of love like that. But now, I see it like that. You're saying that because God loves us with outrageous love, we should love others with reckless love.

You've got me thinking. If my love for Pat is sufficient, then it must be selfless and sacrificial, right? I struggled at the thought at first. But know what? Even if I never see Pat again, I'll pray for her every day. And I'll pray for her mom and dad also.

Doctor, I told you. My folder on Kathy's good news is growing fat with goodies. They'll last me a lifetime. Thank you, thank you.

Love,
Kathy.

Date: 7/3/07
Subject: Kathy's good news
From: Kathy
To: Doctor Wilson

Dear Doctor,

It's me again. I hope you don't mind. Thanks. I think I'm going to be a missionary. Does that surprise you? But I think I wouldn't be a missionary who goes to a far away country. I'll be a missionary right here, at home. My mission field is false starts.

Do you know how many false starts there are in my church alone? My mom and my sister and I may not be the only false starts there, no. I weep any time I think about it. Who's going to tell them how to get out of the trap of a false start?

I'm starting to weep again. So I'll stop here.

Bye,

Kathy.

Subject: Kathy's good news
Date: 7/5/07
From: Doctor Wilson
To: Kathy

Dear Kathy,

I tell you from experience. You're at the right spot. You're

- hearing
- seeing, and
- feeling

the heartbeat of God on the issues. Remember my experience following my Dad's sudden death? [See the attachment to my e-mail dated 4/22/07. It's my personal experience of reconnection to God.]

You remember I said that I climbed trees and rooftops, sang and preached two-minute sermons at dawn? Well, what you're seeing, hearing and feeling was what I saw, heard and felt. "Who would tell them?" rang in my heart night and day. And like you, I also wept for false starts. I still do on and off.

You had said that you and I are kindred spirits. In a sense you're right. I was a false start. So were you. But in another sense, we're different. You were lost in church, and you knew it. That's why you went forward nine times seeking to receive Jesus. The tenth time didn't come because you started Kathy's good news discussions with me. Remember?

Unlike you, I was lost in church but I didn't know it. I was confident that my Christian upbringing, regular church attendance, and being good made me a child of God. Thanks to my Mom who, like you, saw it differently. She didn't take chances. She took steps to lead me into a personal relationship with God. That was how I got out of the trap of false assurance. You remember, don't you?

It's hard to believe, Kathy, but it's true. Most false starts are like me and not like you. They're lost in church but they don't know it.

They don't know because false start gives stubborn false assurance. And left unchallenged and corrected over time, stubborn false assurance immunizes victims to the need to enter a personal relationship with God.

The immunization makes it difficult to get the false starts to see that they're trapped in deception, to admit it, and be willing to do something about it. But it's doable.

Look at me. My Mom got me out. Remember my Dad? I got him out. Look at your mom and sister? You got them out. How? The answer lies partly in reckless love when it doesn't fear to hurt the loved one, like my Mom did,

- to ask the hard question ['Do you know God personally?'] in a safe setting, of course
- to listen carefully to the word and body language answer to that question
- to follow the leading of the Holy Spirit and seize the ripe moment to ask further questions
- to discern where the particular false start is

and tactfully take them to where they should be (like my Mom did for me, and like I did for you).

That was how you and I, false starts in church, got out of that trap and entered a personal relationship with God.

The role of the Spirit in all this is most important. But he uses people like you, my Mom, and me, even when we don't feel he's using us. Give me six days and I'll put together for you an introduction to "The Holy Spirit and the re-created."

I hope I didn't discourage you in your desire to be a missionary here at home? Continue to be open to God on that. He'll make it plain to you in his way and time. I know he will. But meanwhile, Kathy, pray, and continue to pray that you may meet people, who would be willing to listen to your personal experience of Jesus.

That's all we do really. We tell people how Jesus has changed us, showing them how thankful we are that he did. You'll be amazed how many more people would seek you out wanting to hear your story when word begins to get out. I'm praying for you, Kathy.

Always your friend,
Doctor Wilson.

Date: 7/10/07
Subject: Kathy's good news

From: Kathy
To: Doctor Wilson.

Dear Doctor,
    You, discourage me? Never. Everything you say is an en-
couragement to me. I didn't know that a false start leads to false
assurance, and that false assurance immunizes people to the need
to become a child of God until you said it. Knowing it now
doesn't discourage me or scare me away from false starts. Rather,
knowing it has deepened my concern for them.
    But I have a problem. Now, I can't stop thinking about
false starts. I try to push the thought away. It goes and comes
back again. Then, 'Who will tell them?' begins to tick like a
clock in my heart. The ticking hurts. Do you think I'm becom-
ing insane? I hope not.
    Your friend,
    Kathy.

Subject: Kathy's good news
Date: 7/11/07
From: Doctor Wilosn
To: Kathy

Dear Kathy,
    No, no, you're not insane. You're totally normal.
Look at the pain as compassion for false starts. Deep
down in your heart, you desire that they come out of

where you've been, unsure of a personal relationship with God; and be where you are, sure of a personal relationship with God. So I suggest that you don't resist thinking about false starts.

I also suggest that you start a journal. Call it 'Thoughts on false starts.' And date it. Write down the thoughts as they come to you, and date them. On and off, go back and read what you've written down. Your journaling may not be coherent. It's not supposed to be.

But you can recognize a common theme. Highlight it with a marker. And hear what it's telling you.

Now, to the Holy Spirit as I promised you. Actually, Kathy, the Holy Spirit is not new to you. See below what you've said about him (in 'The things that led me [Kathy] to the steps' in your e-mail dated 5/30/07).

But know what? There's one more thing. Six, the Holy Spirit: It was the Holy Spirit who opened my mind to see all those new things in Bible stories I've heard over and over again in Sunday school. Don't you agree? It was he who got me to talk to you at the end of your talks in our church. He was the one who led me to fall in love with Jesus. It was the Holy Spirit who helped me to hear and see myself in the exercise on the steps that led me into a personal relationship with God.

Everything you said there is right-on with the Holy Spirit. What I say in the attached file builds on that.

Your friend,
Doctor Wilson.

Attachment file for 7/11/07 e-mail

The Holy Spirit and the re-created

If anyone could be exempt from the presence and work of the Holy Spirit, it must be our Lord Jesus Christ. Why? Jesus and the Holy Spirit are co-equal with God the Father. Yet, Jesus, God in human form, modeled the presence and work of the Holy Spirit in the clearest, the simplest, and the best way possible.

For example, the life of Jesus in Matthew, Mark, Luke and John shows that Jesus lived in and by the Holy Spirit. Right at the beginning the angel told Mary, "The Holy Spirit will come upon you, and the power of the Most High will overshadow you; therefore the child to be born will be called holy, the Son of God" (Luke 1:35).

Then, Jesus did his public ministry in the Spirit, who came on him at his baptism (Luke 3:21-22). "The Spirit of the Lord is upon me," Jesus said, "to be

- good news to the poor
- release to the captives

- sight to the blind
- freedom to the oppressed" (Luke 4:18-19 para-phrased, compare Isa. 61:1-2).

That's the clearest sign that God the Father didn't exempt even Jesus from, "Not by might, nor by power, but by my Spirit, says the LORD of hosts" (Zech. 4:6).

Unlike us, Jesus knew and could do the Father's will at the right time and place. He's always God, even when he was fetus; and when he was on Mary's lap and on Joseph's shoulder (Luke 2:22-52). But like us, he too submitted to being empowered and led moment by moment by the Spirit. When the Pharisees credited demons instead for that empowerment, Jesus told them they sinned against the Spirit. Such sins have no forgiveness, ever (Matt.12:22-32).

No wonder Jesus was full of love, joy, peace, patience; kindness, goodness, faithfulness, gentleness, and self-control. That's outrageous love spelt out. It's the fruit of the Spirit (Gal. 5:22-23).

No wonder Jesus hung out with prostitutes and tax collectors while society looked down on them and stayed away from them as we do AIDS patients today. He touched and healed lepers when priests put them out of society. And while priests would avoid a corpse like the plague, Jesus touched corpses and raised them to life.

However when Jesus died, he died like all people do. But he resurrected in the Spirit, having a spiritual body with flesh and bones. Then the Father enthroned him Lord over all human and spiritual powers and forces, when he ascended to heaven (Rom. 1:4, Eph. 1:19-23).

The apostles and disciples followed in Jesus' steps. They, in turn, modeled and taught that the recreated

- need to have the Holy Spirit as proof of belonging to Jesus at all (Acts 2:37-39, Rom. 8:9)
- need to be filled (empowered and controlled) with the Holy Spirit to live spiritually (Eph. 5:18-20)
- need to be led moment to moment by the Holy Spirit to be Jesus-like (Rom. 8:14).

Then, the Spirit will help them

- to love God with all their heart (Mark 12:29-30)
- to accept and care for other believers irrespective of their backgrounds (John 13:34-35 compare 1 John 4:19-21)
- to forgive and pray for people who treat them like dirt (Matt. 5:43-48, Rom. 12:9-21).

It was through the Spirit that Jesus and his immediate followers lived a lifestyle made up of

- self-imposed weakness (non-threatening posture)
- childlike trust and dependence on God
- love and prayer.

That lifestyle is the only one Satan and demons and anything that hates God

- can't stand
- can't understand
- can't imitate
- can't overcome.

Therefore, a lifestyle of servanthood, love, prayer and trust and dependence on God under the leadership of the Holy Spirit distinguishes Jesus' followers. That lifestyle also protects them in a way nothing else can.

Date: 7/14/07
Subject: Kathy's good news
From: Kathy
To: Doctor Wilson

Dear Doctor,
I don't understand everything you've said about the Holy Spirit. But what I understand makes me love him as I do Jesus. It surprised me that even Jesus needed to have the Holy Spirit. That means we can't do without the Holy Spirit either.
It also surprised me that I had the Spirit without knowing exactly when and how he came to me. While reading your reference in Romans 8, I bumped into this. "For his Holy Spirit speaks to us deep in our hearts and tells us that we are God's

children." (Rom. 8:16 LB)

That explains why I still know that I'm a child of God. And that's how I was able to know and say those things I said in point number six, the portion you quoted in your 7/11/07 e-mail from my 5/30/07 e-mail.

I like this. You said, Satan, demons and anything that hates God can't stand, understand, imitate, or overcome, a lifestyle made up of

- *self-imposed weakness (non-threatening posture)*
- *childlike trust and dependence on God*
- *love*
- *prayer*

under the leadership of the Holy Spirit."

I want to have that lifestyle. Please, tell me how.

Doctor, the teaching on the Holy Spirit is another goodie for life. Thanks.

Your friend,

Kathy.

Subject: Kathy's good news

Date: 7/18/07

From: Doctor Wilson

To: Kathy.

Dear Kathy,

You're welcome any time. Are you surprised that 'Kathy's good news' is about four months old already? Yes, it was born in March, 2007. Lots of things have happened since then, haven't they?

You entered a personal relationship with God on Wednesday (5/9/07). Then, as you know, almost immediately, the relationship between you and your sister went sour when you acted rude to her to get even. But everything returned to normal when you wrote her a letter of apology, remember?

Shortly after that (6/14/07) your mom and sister entered a personal relationship with God when they heard your testimony. Then almost immediately again, you lost your best friend, Pat. Her mom accused you of being a bad influence on Pat. Did you realize that you became a bad influence on Pat only after you'd entered a personal relationship with God?

Losing Pat was crushing. But you overcame when you saw it for what it was. It was suffering persecution for Jesus. Through the teaching on 'Reckless love,' you learned to forgive both Pat and her parents, in spite of themselves. You said so in your e-mail dated (7/1/07).

Right at that time, you started aching for false starts. It appeared you might become a missionary to false starts.

Can you believe that in less than five months you've seen three false starts, that is, you, your mom and your sister, enter a personal relationship with God? You got to know how I, another false start, had entered a personal relationship with God. In addition, you saw how Jesus had led the legion demoniac, Mary Magdalene, Zacchaeus and the Samaritan woman into that relationship.

In the process, you realized that you'd experienced the good news in exactly the way Jesus wants it. The Holy Spirit used new light in the scriptures, and the lives of visibly changed people to help you see Jesus in a clearer and better light. And you fell in love with Jesus.

The process also attracted teaching on the following related topics: Jesus and lostness, people and lostness, and being lost in church; plus temptation, the quiet time, reckless love, and the Holy Spirit.

The overall picture says entering a personal relationship with God is easy. But it's not laidback. It can't be, because a life that gladdens God and rocks heaven ecstatically outrages Satan and everything that hates God. Jesus faced that reality every day of his life, though he was God in human form.

He met open and covered-up resistance and opposition from among the people he related to daily. As God, he could forcibly stop the resistance and opposition. If he did, we couldn't imitate him. Therefore he chose a method anyone, young and old, could copy. This illustrates it.

Jesus gave up equality with the Father and became his servant instead (Phil. 2:5-11; compare Matt. 20:28). To imitate him, we too give up our pride in everything that makes us proud, and learn to be nobodies so we can serve all people without intimidating any (Matt. 10:16, John 17:18, 20:21).

Jesus outrageously loved people, the good and the bad alike. We imitate him through recklessly loving people including those who treat us like dirt. Meaning we give barrels of love where it's normal to ration a teaspoonful of it (John 13:34-35; compare Matt. 5:43-48)

Jesus prayed to maintain his submission to God, and his trust and dependence on his Father (Hebrews 5:7-10). Similarly we pray to sustain our submission to God, and our dependence on God (Acts 4:23-31). Jesus was Spirit-led moment by moment (Luke 4:18-19, John 1:29-34, Rom. 1:4). So must we (Rom. 8:9, 14 and Eph. 5:18).

That was how Jesus lived to please God, the Father. At the same time, that was how he remained genuine and authentic. And that was how Satan and demons and hostile Pharisees (people who hated God's interference in their lives) couldn't overcome him.

In exactly the same way, we will please God and be genuine. Then we also will overcome Satan and demons, and everything that provokes us to forget that we're children of God and live like people without God.

All that gives us a way of life made up of

- willingness to be nobodies for Jesus' sake
- trust and dependence on God
- love,
- prayer, and
- being Spirit-led.

That way of life contradicts and appalls the world's way of life that's made up of defiance, force, greed, selfishness, and evil ambition.

That's why everything that hates God including Satan and demons

- can't stand
- can't understand
- can't imitate
- can't overcome

our way of life which is at the same time our resistance and overcoming power.

Kathy, my friend, we have indeed come a long way from that Sunday night we sat facing each other in your pastor's office? Looking back, I'm glad I promised not to laugh at you, and I didn't.

More than that, I'm glad 'Kathy's good news' came to life. Through Kathy's good news, I gained three sisters in Jesus, you, your mom, and your sister. For that,

I'm overjoyed. Bravo, Kathy, bravo!
Love,
Doctor Wilson.

Date: 7/25/07
Subject: Kathy's good news
From: Kathy
To: Doctor Wilson.

Dear Doctor,

It took me this long to control myself, to stop weeping so I could write back. Something in your e-mail, I don't know what it is, made me feel I was losing you all of a sudden. But I know better than that. You and I will always be friends. Daddy reminded me about that when he came to my room last night and met me weeping, staring at your 7/18/07 e-mail.

Okay, Doctor, now you can laugh all you want. But know what? You'll be laughing for a different reason. You have made me a missionary to false starts. Believe me. But, of course, I have a lot to learn from you yet on that. You're my mentor, remember?

For now, Doctor, all I can say is, thank you, thank you, thank you. I'm a child of God and I know it. Yes, I do.

Love,
Kathy.

ALSO BY WILSON AWASU

KIM'S CONFESSIONS

Kim thinks she's a true believer. She's a ninth-generation Presbyterian and her church's choir director, to boot. But she's about to learn that belief isn't something you can take for granted.

It all starts when her pastor puts on a seminar called "Radical Growth."

Confronted with challenges to her trust in the Lord, Kim puts up a strong resistance. After all, she's done all the right things, knows all about the Bible; how could she be less than fully trusting in God? But when a pointed example reveals her deeply hidden skepticism, Kim faces the truth she can't ignore.

What follows is a journey of faith and personal discovery that will give Kim a relationship with God she hasn't had in her 43 years. The key is to learn childlike trust in God — a message easier said than done. Along the way, she'll also experience a healing of the grudges, disdain and disrespect she didn't even know she held. And her radical transformation will end up having a larger impact on the church than she could ever have imagined...

Eye-opening and moving, Kim's Confessions explores the real meaning of belief. Part spiritual history, part guidebook, it's a must-read for anyone seeking a deeper relationship with God.

Learn more at: www.outskirtspress.com/WilsonAwasu

CPSIA information can be obtained at www.ICGtesting.com
Printed in the USA
BVOW031647150712

295223BV00001B/1/P